Presented to:

From:

Date:

God Said What?
Devotional Book for Teens

Tina Toler

All Scripture passages are taken from the New International Version.

God Said What?
A Devotional Book for Teens
ISBN 1448633915
Copyright @ 2009 by Tina Toler
320 West Hay Street
Whiteville, NC 28472

All rights reserved under International Copyright Law. Contents and/or cover may not be reproduced in whole or in part in any form without the express written consent of the Author.

In Loving Memory of:

Mike Todorovich (1921-1995) my grandfather who taught me people can change; who you were in the past doesn't matter, it's who you are now that does.

Ward Lynn Duncan (1915-1999) my grandfather, for whom my son Jacob was named, taught me more than will fit in this small space. From him I learned my love of camping, love for my family, what it means to be loved unconditionally, corny jokes, silly songs, and how to approach the end of life with gratitude for what you had and grace in saying good-bye.

Dorothy Emelie Kinser Todorovich (1921-1991) my grandmother, for whom my daughter, Emily Marie, was named, prayed for me when others thought I was hopeless. She taught me to persevere through the storms of life and know the sun will once again shine. Her last words to me, "your baby is a blessing" are an attribute to her intense insight into life and God and to her tendency to always be right.

Soldiers killed in action and all military personnel: my many thanks go out to each one over the course of our great nation for their selfless, heroic sacrifices. These are the men and women who give me the freedom to write this book, and give you the freedom to read it. To all the families who have loved ones away or loved ones who have been killed in the line of duty, my prayers and thanks are with you always.

Special Thanks to:

My four children, Emily, Eric, Jessica and Jacob: You are the love of my life, my reason for everything I do. Thank you for your support and encouragement during the writing of this book. I love you so much!

To my "other" children, Brandi, Marc, Alexander (who looks just like me), Brooke, Jaylen, Brett (who calls me Moo-Moo) and all the others who practically live at my house: I love ya'll so much and am very blessed you have become part of my family.

Larry Keel, my better half: Thank you for helping me out so much with the kids, all the cups of coffee and especially your love and support. I love you.

Esther Margie Anderson, my mom: Thanks for listening to me when I feel like I am worthless, for encouraging me not to give up and for all your editing help. I love you.

Michael David Todorovich, my brother and best friend: Words can not express my thoughts, feelings, and thanks for you. If I were to write it all down it would be the entire book. You are the one who stands by me when I am ready to fall, the one who knows I am practically insane but loves me anyway and the one who makes me laugh no matter how much I am hurting. Everyone needs a brother and friend like you and it doesn't hurt that you gave me two incredible nieces! You taught me although we started as dirty pieces of coal, we can reach our dreams and be diamonds, so "Shine on you crazy diamond" (Pink Floyd).

Yvonne Duncan, my grandmother: Thank you for loving me unconditionally and for always being on my side. I love you Mama.

Brandi and Jonathan, Emily, Eric, and Jessica: Thank you for helping me with pictures! I couldn't have done it without you.

And most importantly, God: Thank You for everything I have in my life, for my lessons I have learned, for my children and family, and for the gift of writing. Thank You mostly for my gift of salvation, which I receive only through Your grace. Without You I am nothing, have nothing and can do nothing.

NOTE FROM THE AUTHOR — 11

THE SIGNATURE — 12

THE TEN COMMANDMENTS — 13

The Ten Commandments — 14
"You Shall Have No Other God's Before Me" — 15
"You Shall Not Make for Yourself an Idol" — 17
"You Shall Not Misuse the Name of the Lord Your God" — 18
"Remember the Sabbath" — 19
"Honor Your Father and Mother" — 22
"You Shall Not Murder" — 23
"You Shall Not Steal" — 25
"You Shall Not Give False Testimony against Your Neighbor" — 27
"You Shall Not Covet" — 29

SELF IMAGE — 31

Set Apart by God — 32
In God's Image — 38
Leaving Behind the Old — 41
Unseen Beauty — 43

WHAT IS LOVE? — 45

What Is Love Anyway? — 46
Love is Patient — 47

Love is Kind	49
Love Does Not Envy	51
Love Does Not Boast and is Not Proud	53
Love is Not Rude	55
Love is Not Self-Seeking	57
Love is not Easily Angered	58
Love Keeps No Record of Right or Wrong	60
Love Does Not Delight in Evil	61
Love Rejoices with Truth	63
Love Protects, Trusts, Hopes and Perseveres	65

PARENTS — 67

Parents!	68
Responsibility and Life Lessons	69
Parents Know Best	71

GIVING TO OTHERS — 74

Giving to Others	75
Becoming a Servant	76
Give Generously	78
Giving to the Oppressed	80
Using Your Gifts	83
Offering Help to Other Believers	85
Praying for Others	86
Hospitality	88

TEMPTATION — 90

Temptation	91
Jesus Understands	92
Watch for Temptation	94

JUDGMENT — 96

Judgment	97
Judge Not	98
Passing Judgment	100
Slander and Rumors	102
Judgment from Others	104

HOPE IN GOD — 106

Hope in God	107
The Shepherd and the Sheep	108
Whom Shall I Fear?	110
Joy through Trials	112
Peace with God	114
"Pray Also for Me"	116

FORGIVENESS — 117

Forgiveness	118
Asking God's Forgiveness	119
Forgiving and Letting Go of Bitterness and Anger	121
Forgiving Others	123
Forgiving Yourself	125

SAVED BY GRACE — 127

For God so Loved the World — 128

The Way, the Truth and the Life — 129

Saved by Grace — 130

Salvation in Jesus Christ — 132

About the Author — 134

Note from the Author

Hello to all my new friends,

The creation of this book has been long and tedious. When God first talked to me about writing this type of book, I of course, argued with Him. I couldn't figure out why He would want me to do this. Surely there was someone else better qualified; someone who had a doctorate degree in religion or was a better Christian. So I told God how I felt, expecting Him to realize I was right and He was wrong.

He didn't listen!

He kept pushing and nagging me. I would wake up at night thinking about it, think about it in the grocery store, while driving; I thought about it at the most inconvenient and irritating times. I tried explaining to God I didn't have a religion degree, nor did I have a journalism degree. I had no experience and was not qualified for this endeavor. Besides, although I am a Christian, I have made more than my share of mistakes and still do. Apparently God knew since I have made so many mistakes and been through so much, I could help others.

I finally accepted that arguing with God wasn't getting me anywhere and He definitely knows more than I do, so I gave in. A book was at last born.

My goal isn't to become rich (although that *would* be nice), but to help teens deal with issues I have faced in my life and that my children now face. Knowing my own children respond better and listen more intently when told a story instead of being "preached at", I decided fictional stories may help gain attention more than words written in text book style.

Picking out the Bible verses was difficult. There are so many wonderful verses that teach valuable lessons it was hard to narrow it down. Leaving some of them behind was painful, but I didn't want "Bible overload". I also left out parts of the Devotional I would have liked to add, but once again I decided to keep it short. Maybe, if this book inspires and helps others, I will one day write a follow up, so please contact me if you are interested in another book.

Although the stories in this book are fictional unless otherwise noted, the circumstances are real. As my kids and their friends have opened up and discussed some very private issues, I have truly listened, not just with my ears but with my heart. In my own life, I have experienced many of the obstacles, confusions and fears mentioned here. If my experiences and pain help even one teen, then it has been worth it all.

My hope for this book is to teach you more about yourself and help you grow closer to God. He is truly amazing and loves you more than you will ever be able to comprehend. His love, grace, forgiveness, and healing will be freely given to you. All you have to do is ask.

Many prayers and much love to you,
Tina

The Signature

The morning Star, the last one seen,

Defies the order of night,

But in defiance, overstays his welcome,

To be consumed by heaven's Light.

Not merely once, but countless performed,

This harrowing shadow play.

A constant reminder, to every age,

That Victory precedes each day.

                              Michael Tildsley, Jr.

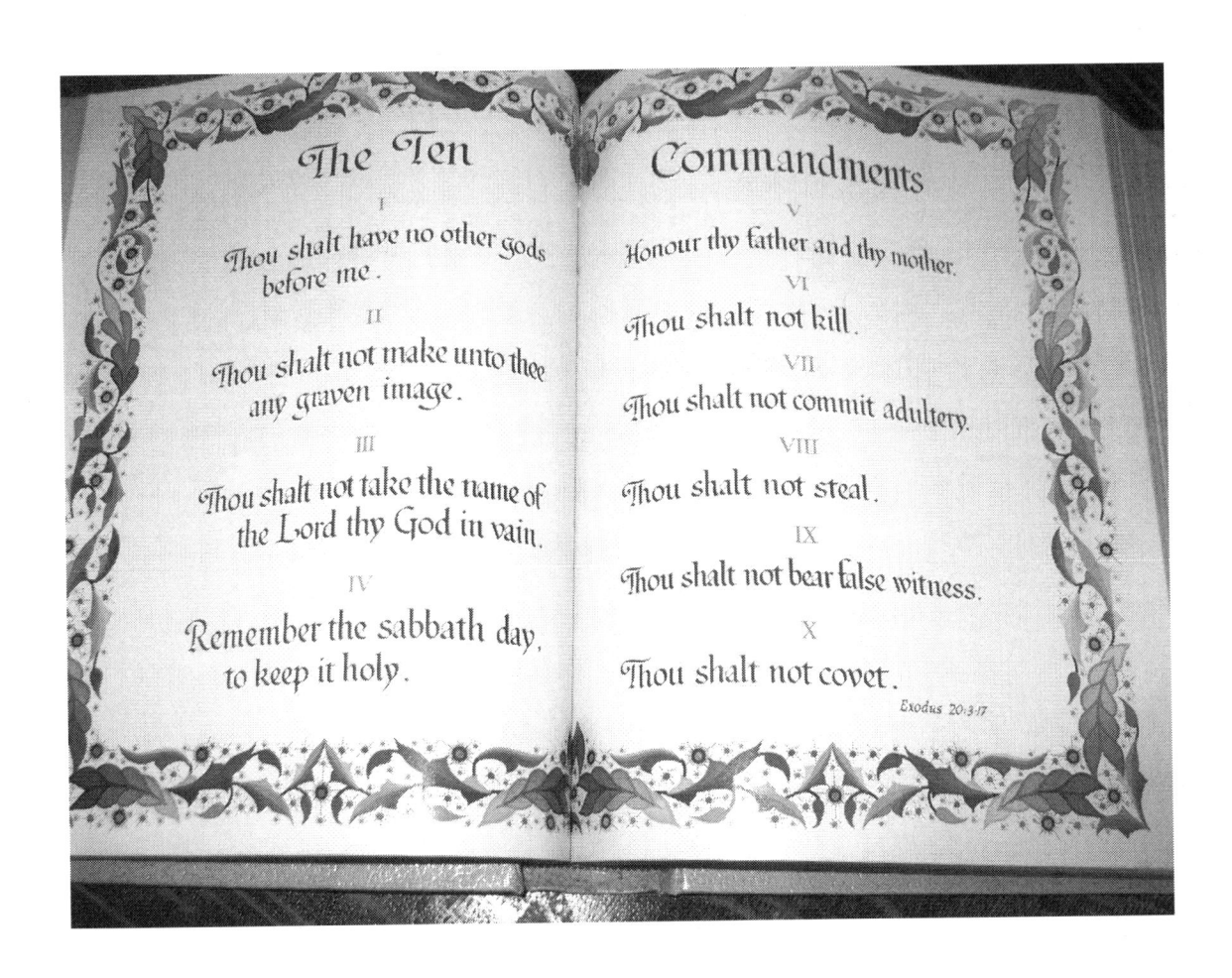

The Ten Commandments

The Ten

I

Thou shalt have no other gods before me.

II

Thou shalt not make unto thee any graven image.

III

Thou shalt not take the name of the Lord thy God in vain.

IV

Remember the sabbath day, to keep it holy.

Commandments

V

Honour thy father and thy mother.

VI

Thou shalt not kill.

VII

Thou shalt not commit adultery.

VIII

Thou shalt not steal.

IX

Thou shalt not bear false witness.

X

Thou shalt not covet.

Exodus 20:3-17

The Ten Commandments

Do you ever feel like you have no clue what you are doing? Like you aren't sure what is right and what is wrong? I think everyone feels that way sometimes.

Wouldn't it be nice if life were like a new cell phone and came with a user's manual telling you what to do and what not to do? Like, "don't push this button it is a sin" or "push this key for understanding". That would be awesome.

Well, guess what. Life does come with a user's manual. They are called "the Ten Commandments" and they are straight from God. He gave them to Moses thousands of years ago to guide His people in the right direction and they are still our manual today.

Every generation is different in some way than the one before. New problems are generated and new issues must be dealt with. Many times it's a wait and see approach and sometimes it's a hope for the best situation. But one thing is still the same. God will never change and his commandments still hold true for us today as they did for those many generations ago.

As you read them, think about how to apply them in your life. Really think about them and let God's word guide you through.

"You Shall Have No Other God's Before Me"

Bible Verse: {God said} "You shall have no other gods before me." Exodus 20:3

Something to Think About: Being the star quarterback on the football team, Seth was surrounded by trophies, certificates and game footballs. His entire room was covered with photos magazine clippings and posters of pro football players. Football was his life.

His freshman year, Seth broke his foot in the first practice of the year and had to sit the bench. He hated every minute of it, but found strength through God and his fellow teammates and endured the torture of watching the others play. He was the team's biggest cheerleader, and he couldn't wait to get back out onto the field.

As he was recovering from foot surgery he prayed constantly, "God, please heal my foot and let me play ball again. You have given me the gift of being fast and knowing what to do on the field. Please don't let me lose that gift."

God answered his prayer and by mid-season his sophomore year he was back on the field. He prayed often, thanking God for healing him and allowing him to play again. As the games passed and his fame grew, he prayed less often. He told himself he was just getting busy and he knew God understood. At first, he really was busy, but never too busy to find a few minutes to pray, even if in the shower. Eventually, he even gave that up.

By his junior year, he was the star, almost unheard of at the school. Most stars were in their senior year and had at least three good years of high school football experience. Seth missed his first year and he was a junior, so he only had one good year of experience, but he was so great it didn't matter. He led the team to an undefeated season and to the state championships, which he won in the last thirty seconds of the game. His trophy case was full and everyone loved him. Even Mayor Resley thought of Seth as a big star. When he went out for a burger, he didn't have to pay for it. He got into movies free. Everyone in town thought he was a hero and he got the royal treatment.

His senior year was even better. Talent scouts from three major schools watched him play and he was offered three different full ride scholarships. He knew it was because he was awesome. After all the accolades from everyone at school and the whole town, Seth forgot all about God. He stopped going to church and left his church youth team without a second thought. For him, football had become his god.

When most people read "thou shall have no other gods" they assume it means something like Buddha or Zeus from Greek mythology. It does mean that, but it means so much more. Anything or anyone that becomes more important to you than God becomes your god. It could be a football team, a celebrity, money, clothes, movies…anything. It is definitely ok to have other things in your life, in fact, God wants you to. You just cannot put it before God. Always put Him first in everything you do and never forget to thank Him.

Prayer: Dear Heavenly Father, Please forgive me for the times I put other things or people before You. Sometimes I just get caught up in life as a teen and forget what is important. Help me realize when I am doing it and help me to change. Lord, You are amazing and worthy of all my praise and attention. Please help me remember that.
~Amen

"You Shall Not Make for Yourself an Idol"

Bible Verse: {God said} "You shall not make for yourself an idol in the form of anything in heaven or on the earth beneath or in the waters below. You shall not bow down to them or worship them." Exodus 20:4

Something to Think About: Luna loved crystals ever since she was a little girl. She thought they were the most beautiful stone in the world. When light filtered through them, rainbows of magnificent colors filtered through, covering her room with rich radiance.

As she grew up, Luna researched crystals. She was astounded when she found that in ancient times people believed her favorite object had healing powers. She found the magic associated with them spell binding and cherished them even deeper. Over time she began to believe in their magic and worshipped them. Each one had its special place of honor on her dresser with a shrine built around it. She believed in their power so strongly that she gave up her trust in medicine, relying only on her crystals. When she had a headache she slept with one under her pillow. When she had cramps, she rested one on her tummy, waiting for the magical power to release her pain.

When her grandmother became seriously ill, Luna did not turn to God. She didn't ask Him to heal Granny nor did she believe He could. Her faith lied in her smallest, most cherished crystal, brought over from Uganda by her Aunt Mickie. When Granny did not recover and died from cancer, she blamed God. "God, it's all Your fault!" She yelled. "The crystals would have worked if you wouldn't have butted in and kept them from it! How dare you!"

Luna was worshipping her crystals as an idol instead of worshipping God. She put them first in her life and believed in *their* power, not God's. It is so important not to have idols, whether they are pictures, books, crystals or even people. God is the only One you should be worshipping and believing in.

Prayer: Dear Heavenly Father, help me see if I am worshipping any idols instead of You. Forgive me for any times I may have and I haven't even realized it. Help me always put You first and only worship You.
    ~Amen

"You Shall Not Misuse the Name of the Lord Your God"

Bible Verse: {God said} "You shall not misuse the name of the Lord your God, for the Lord will not hold anyone guiltless who misuses His name." Exodus 20:7

Something to Think About: In a fit of anger, Jennison could not control herself and began screaming, "God, this sucks. I hate this. God d*** it". She had never used language like this before and neither had her parents. She knew it was wrong and knew she was using God's name in vain. Instead of using His name in honor, she was using it in disgust and hatred.

It's easy to get caught into the trap Jennison found herself in. The world seems to be using God's name all the time. You hear it in the hallways at school, on the bus ride home. You hear it in movies and read it in books. You become immune to its meaning and view it as just another saying. It becomes as insignificant as saying, "Man, this stinks." However, God does not feel that way. He deserves more from us than this. He deserves His name to be respected and honored.

Sometimes it's really difficult and you may occasionally slip. I know I have and my daughter has. If you do, don't think you are a horrible person who is going straight to hell. Instead, take some time alone and pray about it. Ask God to forgive you for using His name in vain and ask Him to help you remember next time. He will forgive you; after all, He is God!

Prayer: Dear Heavenly Father, I ask You to please forgive me for the times I may slip up and use Your name in vain. I know it is wrong and I know Your name deserves nothing but respect and praise. Please help me when my anger gets the best of me. Keep my thoughts clean and pure and keep me from thinking the wrong words. Teach me to use Your name only in praise and with respect.

~Amen

"Remember the Sabbath"

Bible Verse: {God said} "Remember the Sabbath day by keeping it holy. Six days you shall labor and do all your work but the seventh day is a Sabbath to the Lord your God." Exodus 20:8-10

Something to Think About: After Michael graduated high school, he took a summer job working as a legal assistant for a major law firm in town. He was going to school for pre-law to prepare for law school and this was a huge step in his career. The job not only helped him with his resume, but also paid very well and he was able to help pay for his college tuition and take some of the burden from his family.

During a strenuous and important case, the lawyers worked ten to twelve hours a day, seven days a week. They expected their assistants to do the same. Michael didn't mind the long hours, in face, he loved them. He was learning more than he imagined and the overtime helped pad his savings account. He did hate working on Sundays. Sunday's were his Sabbath and he knew God commanded a Sabbath day.

"Mr. Ritter, may I speak with you?" Michael asked his boss.

"Sure, what's up Michael?" Mr. Ritter answered.

Michael took a deep breath, "Mr. Ritter, I love working here and I am learning so much. I don't mind the long hours at all, but I would really appreciate it if I could take Sunday's off."

"You want all Sunday's off or just this one?" his boss asked.

"I want all Sunday's off. See, I am Christian and I believe in observing the Sabbath and not working." Michael stated with confidence.

"I see. Well, Michael, you are doing an amazing job here and I respect your position. However, we are really in a rush on this and time is of essence." Mr. Ritter said sympathetically.

"I just don't feel right working and missing church Sir. It goes against all I believe in." Michael said sadly.

"Michael, I am a Christian as well and I hate when we have to work Sunday's and I miss church. Last week our youth group led the service and I missed watching my daughter sing two songs. But it's something that has to be done sometimes. I am really sorry, but I just can't give you the time off".

Michael thought a lot about what Mr. Ritter said. He decided he was going to quit his job, even though without it he would not have been able to start college in the fall. That night, he called his minister and spoke to him about it.

"Rev. Garrett, I have a problem maybe you can help me with." Michael told him.

"Sure Michael, you know I am always here for you. What's up?" Rev. Garret asked.

Michael explained the situation to him and Rev. Garrett listened intently. After Michael finished, Rev. Garret gave his opinion.

"Michael, what is my job?" asked Rev. Garrett.

"Um, well, you are our preacher." Michael said with confusion.

"Right. And what do I do as your preacher?" Rev. Garrett asked, wanting Michael to think deeper.

"You visit the sick when they are in the hospital, you visit nursing homes and shut-ins and you preach on Sundays."

"Exactly. My Job is to preach and I do it on the Sabbath. Do you remember the sermon from last Sunday? I read from Mark, chapter one verses 21 through 34."

"Yeah, I remember. You were talking about Jesus driving out demons and healing Simon's mother in law right?" Michael asked.

"Right. And do you remember why that particular day had meaning?"

"Nah, not really. I mean, the healings were miraculous but I don't remember anything about that particular day." Michael admitted.

"It was a Sabbath. Jesus healed on Sabbath, something that was supposed to be forbidden. Sometimes you have to do things that day that you don't want to. We have to care for our families and sometimes work does have to come first."

"But, what about God? Does He understand?"

"Yeah, God understands but only if you don't forget Him. Take time to pray and remember Him. Don't let the day be only work. Even if you have to have a short prayer and read a few Bible verses on your coffee break or pray on the way to and from work, remember Him. Do that every day, in fact. God is amazing. Trust in Him to understand and lead you on your way." Rev. Garrett told him.

"Thanks. I appreciate it." Michael replied.

It would be nice if life worked around our schedules and we could always hold the Sabbath as a personal day. Many years ago people could do that, but even then people had to eat and clean up their messes and animals had to be fed. Today, things are hectic. Many times parents work six or seven days a week and the only time to get anything done around the house is on Sunday's. Sometimes your boss demands you work on Sunday's and you either work or lose your jobs, and jobs are harder and harder to come by.

If you are faced with working on the Sabbath, whether it is on a Saturday or Sunday, pray about it. Talk to God about your dilemma and let Him guide you. For some, the choice will be simple. Some will say, 'I have to work' and some will say, 'It's just not worth it'. For some of you, however, the decision will be more difficult. Remember, Jesus understands how life has changed and understands your responsibilities. Just don't forget God!

Prayer: Dear Heavenly Father, please help me when I have to make a decision about working on the Sabbath. Help me make the best decision so I meet my responsibilities but also honor You.
    ~Amen

"Honor Your Father and Mother"

Bible Verse: {God said} "honor your father and your mother, so that you may live long in the land the Lord your God is giving you." Exodus 20:12

Something to Think About: "Mom told me I couldn't go to the party," whined Sable. "It's just not fair. Everyone is going to the party and I have to sit at home. I hate her sometimes."

"I know what you mean. My mom told me I couldn't go either," Lena stated.

"I am going to be there. Mom and Dad go to bed by ten and I figure the party's just getting started about then. I am going to sneak out and Reba is going to pick me up around the corner. We can meet you there too and you can go with us!" Sable said as if it were no big deal.

"I can't sneak out. I will get caught. Mom seems to know everything I do. And even if I didn't get caught, I am sure Ms. Duncan on the corner will see me. That nosey woman sees everything! Besides, I don't want to lie to Mom and Dad. It just doesn't feel right." Lena stated.

"It's no big deal. Just go out the back door and cross through the White's yard to the corner. They are out of town and won't even know. Then Ms. Duncan won't see you." Sable said.

"No, I can't go against what Mom said. Even if I am mad and think it's unfair, I can't lie to them and do what they told me not to," Lena said.

Lena did the right thing. Even though she really wanted to go to the party and was angry and hurt she couldn't; she still respected her parents' decision. That is what God tells us to do. He doesn't tell you to like everything they tell you or to enjoy everything they make you do. He says to respect and honor them.

Prayer: Dear Heavenly Father, Thank You for giving me parents who love me. I know they only want what's best for me, even when I think they are just being unfair. Help me always remember to honor them and respect them.
    ~Amen

"You Shall Not Murder"

Bible Verse: {God said} "You shall not murder". Exodus 20:13

Something to Think About: This is self explanatory and no story is needed. Since you already know anything you could read, I am going a different route on this one. Instead of pointing out how wrong and sinful murder is, something you are certainly aware of, I am going to talk about those who have already committed the crime.

Aster was a twenty four year gang member. He was inducted to the gang at sixteen when he was kicked out of his home for repeated drug use.

One evening, Aster and his "bros" were out on a drug run when the cops showed up. His fellow gang mates ran quickly in different directions, leaving only him and his cousin, Randolph, standing there, facing the police. From the corner of the lot, shots began firing. First, a single, loud rifle shot aimed in the air, a hope to scare the police away. When the scare didn't work, rounds began sailing from every nook and cranny of the lot and old building. The police, who were appropriately armed for battle, began shooting back in self defense.

Aster wasn't a bad kid deep down. He didn't want to hurt anyone. All he wanted was his drugs and to get out of dodge; to run and never be seen. An older man, with a round belly and a bald head, looked squarely into Aster's eyes. "Put your hands behind your head" the officer demanded.

"Come on. I wasn't shooting. Just let me get out of here!" Aster screamed as his cousin stood watching.

Another round of shooting brought his attention to the right side of the lot. He looked at his cousin just in time to see the bullet from another policeman's gun enter his cousin, sending him crushing to the ground.

Rage, fear and hurt welled deep inside Aster. As the officer once again stared at him yelling, "Put your hands behind your head," Aster swiftly grabbed his cousins dropped and loaded gun, pointed it at the officer and shot him in the chest. The officer was not wearing armor and the bullet exploded inside his chest, nicking his heart. The officer fell to the ground, gasping in pain.

Aster ran over to him. "I am so sorry. I never wanted to hurt anyone. I am so sorry," He kept repeating over and over again.

Somehow the officer believed him. Maybe it was the hurt in his eyes or the innocence that shined through despite the harshness of his world. He would never know why, but the officer actually felt Aster's pain.

"Son, you still have a chance. Turn yourself in, repent to God, and truly live. Even though you will be in prison, your life, your true life, will just be beginning. Teach others to avoid drugs and gangs. Give them the chance you never had," the officer said, struggling for each breath. At last, the officer sighed deeply, squeezed Aster's hand, closed his eyes and died.

Reading the story, you know Aster was wrong. You know he committed a crime and also committed a sin. He did not obey the Ten Commandments. This boy is doomed to prison and hell right? Not necessarily.

Although Aster ended up spending twenty years in prison, he began better life only minutes after the officer's death. He turned his attention, love and hope to God. Asking God for mercy and forgiveness, he gave his heart to Jesus and let Him take control. While in prison, Aster wrote letters to teen magazines, schools and churches. After five years, he was able to go to schools with armed guards watching his every move, and speak against drugs, violence and gangs. He received numerous letters from kids telling him they had been approached by gangs or offered drugs, but because of his testimony, they refused. He saved many lives.

Why am I telling this story of a murderer having a happy ending? Because I want you to see God can use your life, no matter how messed up and how bad, for good. Don't think, "I can go out and murder someone and still have a good life" because that isn't what I am telling you. Aster did not know God before the shooting nor had he been taught of God's love, commandments or forgiveness. You have. Once Aster learned of God, he changed his life. Only when your physical life ends is it too late to give your life to God.

Prayer: Dear Heavenly Father, Please help me never be caught in a position where I am tempted to murder. Please help me remember all those who have sinned against you and murdered someone and help me remember to pray and witness to them. Remember them, Father, and lead them to You.
    ~Amen

"You Shall Not Steal"

Bible Verse: {God said} "You shall not steal." Exodus 20:15

Something to Think About: The drug stores had more lip stick colors than Heather could imagine. Shades of pink, red, coral and browns lined the shelves, calling out to the thirteen year old girl.

"Mom, I want one of these. What color do you like?" Heather asked excitedly.

"Heather, you know I think you are too young for lipstick. I will buy you some lightly colored lip gloss, but not lipstick." Her mom replied demandingly.

"Okay" Heather said sadly.

Heather really wanted the electric pink shade. All the girls at school were wearing it, even to church. Why couldn't she? She was too old enough, no matter what Mom thought. Looking around the store to make sure Mom had gone to the other aisle looking at hair color and no employees were around, Heather was working on getting her nerve up. Finally, she picked up a little tube and stuck it in her pocket. No one noticed.

She had never stolen anything before, not even a piece of bubble gum from her sister's stash. She felt bad for what she had done, but told herself it was only a three dollar tube of lipstick and it was no big deal.

When she was in her room studying, she couldn't help but keep thinking about what she had done. She couldn't even muster the courage to open the tube and try it. Crying, she prayed to God for forgiveness. After she prayed, she went to her mom's room.

"Mom, I need to talk to you. Do you have a minute?" she asked.

"Yeah, what's up sweetie?" Mom asked, expecting her to be asking if she could go to a friend's house over the weekend.

"Well, I, um, well, um…" Heather stammered.

"Just tell me. We can deal with it, no matter what." Mom said, knowing something was really wrong.

"Well, at the store today when you wouldn't buy me the lipstick… well, I really wanted it so bad." She began.

Thinking the same topic of Heather being grown up was what was on her daughter's mind, her mom said, "I know. I still don't think you are old enough. When you start high school we will talk about it, but you aren't wearing lipstick until then."

"No Mom. That's not what I mean. I mean, I really wanted the lipstick so bad and I well, I um, I took a tube and stuffed it in my pocket. Here it is" Heather said as she handed her mom the unopened tube of lipstick.

"Heather, you know this is wrong. But since you were honest with me you are in less trouble, but no going out this weekend. And, we are going to the store first thing in the morning and returning this." Mom said.

"Ok," Heather said, relieved for telling the truth.

Sometimes it's easy to pick up something little and think "It's not a big deal", but stealing anything is wrong. Stop and consider what you are doing and if you are tempted to take anything, remember, no matter how large or small, it is stealing.

Prayer: Dear Heavenly Father, Thank You for teaching me right from wrong. Help me avoid temptation and when I am faced with it, help me be strong and do the right thing.
    ~Amen

"You Shall Not Give False Testimony against Your Neighbor"

Bible Verse: {God said} "You shall not give false testimony against your neighbor." Exodus 20:16

Something to Think About: Mary Elizabeth and Jonathan had been friends since the sandbox. They had never gotten into trouble, but that all changed one summer's evening.

"Hey, I have an idea. You know Old Ms. Beatty down the street? The one who likes to bud into everyone's business and yells at us when she thinks we are too loud?" Jonathan asked.

"Yeah, I know her. What's your idea?" Mary Elizabeth replied.

"Well, let's put poison on her petunias she keeps out front of her gate. She always yells at us that our walking on her sidewalk is too close to her flowers. Let's just get rid of them. That will teach her." Jonathan said.

"Yeah, sounds like a plan. Let's do it tonight!" She said excitedly.

That night, they each snuck out of their homes and poisoned old Ms. Beatty's prize petunias. The petunias died within three days. The whole neighborhood was discussing it and wondering who it could be. Finally, Jonathan's dad asked Mary Elizabeth if she had seen anyone, since her window looked right over the yard. Of course, Mary Elizabeth and Jonathan had already concocted a story in case this happened.

"Yeah, I did. I didn't want to say anything because I don't want to get anyone in trouble, but I noticed Jake and Genevon walking back and forth in front of her house a few nights ago. I thought it was weird and they were probably up to something, but they are always so weird I ignored them," She lied.

Genevon and Jake were both punished at home, although they denied doing anything. Elizabeth and Jonathan were never even considered as the perpetrators and got off scott free. They never felt bad about Genevon and Jake, but instead often laughed over how they got them into trouble.

It is wrong to lie, but it is worse to lie and accuse someone of doing something they haven't. False testimony is just that, saying someone has done something they haven't. If you have done something wrong, confess and do not blame someone else.

Prayer: Dear Heavenly Father, Please forgive me for the times I have said something untrue about someone. When I am tempted to place blame on someone else, or spread gossip, please help me stay true to You and do the right thing.
    ~Amen

"You Shall Not Covet"

Bible Verse: {God said} "You shall not covet your neighbor's house. You shall not covet your manservant or maidservant, his ox or donkey, or anything that belongs to your neighbor." Exodus 20:17

Something to Think About: For his sixteenth birthday, Armando's dad bought him a new car. OK, the car was ten years old, had a few rust spots and the radio didn't work, but it was new to Armando. He was so excited he finally had wheels and wasn't stuck relying on his parents to take him everywhere he didn't even mind not having a radio. For the first week, he worked hard and buffed as much rust away as he could and cleaned the interior. He even found an old radio at a junk yard and installed it. The speakers weren't great, but at least he had music.

His best friend, Wilson, who happened to live next door, turned sixteen exactly two months after Armando. Wilson was hoping his dad would get a hint from Armando's dad and buy him an old car too. On his birthday, his dad handed him a set of keys sending Wilson and Armando into a hyper excitement. When they walked outside, instead of seeing a beat up old car, they saw a brand new shiny, candy apple red Jeep was sitting in the driveway. When they looked in the Jeep, they noticed it only had 100 miles on it. They jumped in, ready for a drive and cranked the custom stereo his dad had installed. It was one that had a satellite radio and more speakers than either of them had seen in a car before. The music could be heard all over the neighborhood.

At first, Armando was happy to be riding around with him and enjoyed it, but when he went to school the next day in his junk car that he had loved so much, he felt intense jealousy towards Wilson. It wasn't fair that Wilson got a new, shiny Jeep when he only got an old, beat up car.

Armando became so angry and wanted the Jeep so bad; he wouldn't even talk to Wilson anymore. A friendship that had lasted years was over. Every time he saw the shiny red Jeep pull into a parking space at school or in the driveway next door, he became angrier. He began hating his car. One evening he had enough of the junker. He took off and crashed his car into a power line and totaled it. Luckily he wasn't injured, but after that, he no longer had his own transportation and once again had to rely on his parents.

It is easy to get caught up in the jealousy game. You have wanted something for a very long time and someone else gets it. Or you want a new, cool cell phone with the full keyboard for easier texting and internet service, but you are stuck with a two year old, out of date, embarrassing phone, then your best friend (or in my case, my son) comes home with the exact phone you wanted. It really hurts and it's ok to be disappointed. This commandment does not mean you aren't allowed to want a car like your friends, or a new cell phone like your boyfriends, or new clothes like your cousins. It means, don't want the one they have and don't resent them for having it. Be happy for them instead of turning against them.

Prayer: Dear Heavenly Father, I know there have been times my jealousy has been out of control and I have resented someone for having what I want. I am truly sorry and ask Your forgiveness. Help me learn not to want other's possessions and to be happy for them no matter what.
    ~Amen

Self Image

This is how everyone sees her; beautiful, amazing, wonderful and happy.

This is how she sees herself; ugly, stupid, horrible and miserably unhappy.

Do you see yourself clearly or are you distorted?

Set Apart by God

Bible Verse: The word of the Lord came to me, saying, "Before I formed you in the womb I knew you, before you were born I set you apart." Jeremiah 1: 4-5

Something to think About: At the family dinner one evening, Mr. and Mrs. Ridley bragged on their son, Jonathan.

"I am so proud of you Son," Mr. Ridley announced.

Mrs. Ridley shook her head in agreement and added, "Getting the solo in the Christmas concert is an amazing honor."

"Yeah, I am pretty psyched about it," Jonathan admitted. "But I have to admit, I am worried I can't do everything. I mean, I have basketball finals coming up and being a starter is a lot of pressure so I can't miss a practice or lose concentration, even for a second. Then there are the two solos I have been asked to do for the town Christmas program. I can't let my studies fall behind. I have a 4.0 and I if I keep this up for the rest of this semester and the next I will be valedictorian. I am working on college applications and they have to be perfect. And if all that weren't enough I am scheduled two days a week to volunteer at the Children's Cancer Center to lead a kid's music class. I just don't see how I can handle it all and do a good job at everything. It feels like too much."

"Of course you can, Jonathan. You have always had this much going, but you are so talented and giving and know how to manage your time. You will pull this off perfectly and do a great job at everything," Mrs. Ridley told him.

Janna felt left out. No one asked her about her day, noticed her new shirt her best friend gave her, or seemed to even notice she was at the table. She felt this way all the time at home, like an outsider. Jonathan had all the talent; she had none. Jonathan sang like an angel while she sounded dying goose. He was a born actor; she couldn't even pretend to be sleepy to get out of chores. His room was always spotless; hers looked like a tornado swept through, disrupting every item she had, and like the clothes hamper and her drawers had exploded. Jonathan had a 4.0 average without trying very hard but she had to study constantly to maintain a 3.0.

Janna felt like she was no one. She didn't feel special, loved or like she had a reason to be in the family. In her eyes, she was below average in looks and intelligence, and only had a few close friends, unlike Jonathan. She felt she couldn't do anything correctly and as a result, gave up trying.

The last time she tried to accomplish anything was playing the piano. It was horrible. She could not remember which key was Middle C, could not get her right hand and left hand to coordinate in unison and scales made no sense. After one year, she walked away and never looked back. After that failure, she vowed never to try anything again.

That night when she went into the bathroom, she really looked at herself in the mirror. All she saw was her dull, straight brown hair. How she wished she had wavy hair like Jonathan's girlfriend. The eyes in the mirror stared back at her did not sparkle like her cousin's. Her breasts were small and barely made a dent in her soft t-shirt, unlike the cheerleaders at school. Her pants were too loose around the waist because she was so skinny, but too tight in the back because, in her opinion, her butt was too big. She hated what she saw.

"I hate who I am. I am plain and ugly and have no talent. I can't even pray anymore. I am too ordinary for even God to want anything do with me. I mean, why would he? I have no talent to offer Him. I don't even want to spend time with me, why would other kids at school and why would God?" Janna fell asleep crying.

The next day, she dressed in a ragged pair of old sweat pants that had a tea stain on the front leg, an oversize sweatshirt that was faded to a gross green and didn't even bother brushing her long hair. She just pulled it up into a pony tail. She felt ugly and depressed and just didn't care.

No one at school noticed how down she was. To them she was meaningless; almost invisible. The only time anyone spoke to her was to ask her to pass their congratulations to her brother, or to yell at her to hurry up and get out of their way. She wanted nothing more than to disappear, and secretly in the darkest parts of her mind, began forming a plan to do just that.

When she got home from school, her only plans were to take a long hot bubble bath, put on her pajamas and work on devising her plan of escape from the world.

Walking through the door, she was greeted by her mother.

"Hey, Sweetie. How was your day?"

"It was okay I guess," she replied without feeling. How could she tell her mother it had been horrendous? She couldn't tell her she hated life, hated school and just wanted it to end. She certainly couldn't allow her mother to see the pain in her soul and her plans; she would only stop it to save embarrassment for the family, not because she loved her. At least, that is what she told herself.

"That's good. I have made some home made chocolate chip cookies and hot chocolate. Come in the kitchen and we will have some. Then, I need you to finish your homework as quickly as possible. We have to be at the Children's Center at six."

"Why do I have to go?" Janna asked. She hated going to the Center. It was filled with sick kids and smelled strong, like ammonia. Besides, she had other plans tonight.

"Because I have volunteered you to run the Children's Church tonight. Allison has the flu and had to cancel and they couldn't find a replacement in such short notice."

"Mom, that's so unfair. You know I hate going there!" Janna screamed.

"I know, but I think you need to get out of the house more. Besides, I am your mother and you do as I say. That's the end of it. Now eat your cookies, do your homework and change into something more appropriate." Her mom wasn't mad at her, but was worried. Janna had been hiding out in the house for months. She knew something was wrong, but Janna refused to admit it. She couldn't just sit around and watch her little girl spin into a depression so deep she couldn't be rescued; she had to push her forward and give her things to do.

Janna ate only one cookie then excused herself. She went to room but didn't take her homework out of her book bag. What was the use? She was failing Algebra anyway, why even try?

After taking a shower and putting on jeans a sweater, Janna came back down stairs.

"I'm ready."

"Good, you look great. Let's go."

At the center that evening, Janna helped the kids color pictures. One little girl sat in the corner alone. Her hair had fallen out and her bald head seemed to be a billboard proclaiming, "Hey, I have cancer." There was no color in her pale cheeks and her clothes hung on her like they belonged to someone much older and larger. Janna's heart went out to her.

"Hi, I am Janna."

"Hi Janna. I am Michaela. I am ten years old." Despite the girl's apathetic appearance, her voice was strong and almost magical, reminding Janna of an angel.

"I have cancer. That's why I am bald." Michaela saw the reaction in Janna's eyes and added, "It's not the really bad kind like some of the kids have. I am probably not going to die. I am taking treatments and the doctors think it will kill all the bad cancer inside me."

Although most of the kids had bald heads, they were sporting cute, stylish hats in all sorts of fashion that drew away from the tale-tell signs. Most of the boys wore ball caps with their favorite team's logo. Some of the girls wore adorable pink ball caps they had decorated themselves. They had yellow and red flowers, ribbons, lace and some sparkly glitter. Janna couldn't help but notice Michaela was the only little girl without a hat.

"I am glad you will be alright," Janna said as she tried her best to give a reassuring smile. "Wow, some of these kids have great hats. Wonder if they would make me one?"

"I am sure they would love to, but why do you want one?"

"Because they are really cute. Why don't you have one? Do you not like caps?"

"I love caps, but my parents did have the money to bring me in a plain one to decorate. All the art supplies are donated to the facility, but no one thought to bring in hats. Maybe one day I will get one."

"Tell you what. I will come back tomorrow and bring us two pink ball caps and you and I will decorate them together. Does that sound good?" Janna hadn't looked forward to anything in a long time, but honestly couldn't wait to come back and help make a hat for Janna.

"Yeah it does, but why do you want one? Do you have cancer and are going to loose your hair too?" Janna asked innocently.

"Um, no, that's not it. I am just so plain and ugly and I don't have any talent. No one even notices I am around and if I disappear no one would miss me. I don't know if I want to the hat so people will actually notice me or so they can't see me. I know I just want one," Janna confessed.

Michaela concentrated on her coloring for a few moments, then looked at Janna. Her eyes were filled with wisdom of an adult instead of an innocent child.

"Janna, are you a Christian?"

"Yes I am, well at least I was. I'm not so sure now. I think God has forgotten about me and doesn't want anything to do with me because I am not special like my brother."

"That's crazy! God doesn't care about things like that. And He never forgets anyone. God made you who you are for a reason. You may think you don't have talents, but maybe He just hasn't showed them to you yet. Not everyone has to do big things to please God. Sometimes just taking time to color with a girl who has cancer is huge in God's eyes. Believe me, not everyone does that."

"Maybe, but I am still just really plain."

"That's just what you see. God sees something different. We are all special and beautiful to Him. Remember, we are created in God's image, so if you say you are ugly and plain you are calling Him ugly and plain. And who knows, maybe God wants you to feel like this so one day you can help someone else who is struggling. Or maybe He doesn't want you involved in big things right now so you can concentrate more on Him. We sure don't know what God's plans are, do we?" Michaela explained.

"Hmm, maybe, but I don't know. I mean, I am nothing special." Janna just couldn't get it through her mind that Michaela was right.

"Well, I know God made you and He loves you, so you are special. Hey, did you know that before Jesus started teaching others about God He was plain? I mean, think about it. He was just a carpenter, a guy who built tables and chairs. He didn't have a designer signature series, or whatever they call it. He wasn't terribly handsome and didn't sing in the choir or wear robes of silk. He was just Him. And He was okay with that because that is how God made Him," Michaela told her. "And look at me. I am nothing special to look at, I am even bald! My foster parents don't have the money to get me clothes that fit so I wear my foster sister's hand me downs. But I know I am not plain or ugly. I am beautiful to God. And so what if I don't sing like Carly or play the guitar like James? That doesn't make me not special. I am still God's child, and so are you."

Michaela and Janna's conversation was interrupted with the sweet song of the piano.

"Are you still coming tomorrow to make hats?" Michaela asked when she realized it was time for Janna to leave.

"Of course. And I will start coming to see you at least two times a week if you don't mind."

"I'd like that a lot."

"See ya tomorrow, Michaela. And thanks."

The next morning, Janna wore jeans she received for her birthday but hadn't worn before. She felt they showed off her behind too much, but decided now she looked good in them. She felt brave and special after talking with Michaela and even put on her new bright red cashmere sweater, wore make up and used hot rollers to make her hair full and bouncy. When she looked into the full length mirror she thought she actually looked pretty good. She didn't care what other kids thought, only what she thought.

"Janna, you look great," Jonathan said as they headed out the door for school.

Janna's mom nodded in agreement. A huge smile spread across her face as she thought, 'my baby girl is going to be alright!"

Everyone feels like Janna at some point. It's so easy to compare yourself to the models on television and in the magazines, and even to your peers and siblings. Many times you may feel you don't have as much to offer God as someone else does, but that isn't true. God doesn't ask you to be better than someone else or to sing or dance or act or to play a musical instrument. All He asks is that you love others and are the best you that you can possibly be. He made you exactly as you are. He knew what you were going to be before your mom and dad even considered having you. You are special, because God planned YOU!

Prayer: Dear Heavenly Father, when I feel like I am nothing and have nothing to give, please remind me I am special. Thank You for making me who I am and for having plans for me before I was even conceived. Thank You for loving me as I am and wanting good things for me. I am sorry I doubt myself, because when I doubt myself I doubt You. Keep me strong in You and help me become the person You want me to be.
~Amen

In God's Image

Bible Verse: So God created man in his own image, in the image of God He created him; male and female He created them. Genesis 1:27

Something to Think About: Cassie, a sixteen year old, started her junior year of High School with dread instead of excitement like her other friends. Instead of looking forward to seeing friends she hasn't seen all summer, she dreaded it. Her mother begged her to go shopping for new school clothes, but Cassie has no interest.

"Cassie, come on. I am offering you a brand new wardrobe for school, complete with shoes, accessories and purses," her mother begged.

"Mom, I said I don't want to go." Cassie yelled. Nothing her mother could say would make her change her mind.

"Okay," her mom said in frustration. "If you change your mind, the offer is still good"

"Thanks, but I won't."

In her room alone, Cassie stood a long time in front of the full length mirror. She saw a short, skinny girl who had the figure of a young boy. Her waist was so tiny her pants barely stayed up. She looked at her backside and thought there was nothing at all there to fill out the seat of her pants. Underneath her t-shirt there were no mounds, not even small ones. No wonder the kids at school called her "skinny Minnie", "Ironing board" and "broomstick." She didn't want to be fat, but certainly didn't want to look anorexic.

She remembered the last day of school. She had a huge crush on Tony. He was tall, blonde and a football quarterback. He was all she thought about. His bright blue eyes seemed to be etched into her memory and her heart.

After two months of him totally ignoring her, he stopped her in the hallway.

"Hey, Cassie. How are you?"

"I'm okay," she replied nervously.

"Um, I have a joke for ya. Wanna hear it?"

"Sure!" She was so excited. She knew Tony had a great sense of humor and he and his friends were always goofing off. She took him wanting to joke with her as a great sign of good things yet to come.

"Okay, if you had no feet, would you wear shoes?"

"Well, no I wouldn't. There would be no point would there?" She was confused. Surely this had a funny punch line, but she wasn't seeing where this was going.

"Then why do you wear a bra?" He began laughing hysterically as he walked off. His friends had walked up right before the punch line and were now holding their stomachs, laughing.

Cassie had never felt so bad in her entire life. She went to the nurse's station, explaining she was sick and asked Ms. Niles to call her mom.

Since that day, she had lost interest in wearing stylish clothing. She knew in her heart she was ugly and clothes wouldn't change that.

At last, Saturday morning rolled around and Cassie went to her grandmother's. Nana always made her feel special.

While they were taking hot, gooey cookies out of the oven, Nana took the opportunity to talk.

"Cassie, what's going on? Your mom said you don't want to get new clothes. Now, I have never in my entire life known a girl who would pass up an opportunity like that. Talk to me."

"Look at me, Nana. I am skinny as a pole. My hair is too curly and my eyes are huge, like bugs. All the other girls have great figures, but look like I am still eight. I look horrible in anything I wear, so why bother?" Cassie admitted.

"Well, I know I am getting old, but I am not blind. That's not what I see. I see a very beautiful girl who was made to be the image of God. If you are ugly, then God is ugly, and honey, God ain't ugly!" Nana told her without sympathy.

"I am too ugly. I look like a train wreck!"

"Cassie, you read the Bible. You believe in God's Word and know He is honest and true and means what He says. The Bible tells us we are created in His image. You are exactly like God made you. You are His image and the love inside you shines brightly." Nana said.

"Then why do the kids at school make fun of me?"

"Honey, kids are cruel. There have always been kids like that, even when I was growing up. I used to get picked on because I rode the ugliest dinosaur to school."

Cassie giggled. "Nana, be serious."

"Okay, okay, but I made you smile! Anyway, kids do it for different reasons. Some do it because they feel bad about themselves and want others to feel just as bad. Some do it because they are jealous and want to bring you down. Some do it because they think it makes they look cool. And some are just plain mean."

"It's just not fair."

Nana thought for just a moment before responding. "Cassie, life isn't fair. It isn't fair you grandfather had to battle cancer. It isn't fair that your Uncle Tom's wife left him for another man. It isn't fair my first baby died when she was only two weeks old. There are always things that will happen that isn't fair. But sweetie, you aren't being fair to yourself or to God when you listen to the mindless put down's of other kids. Don't let them mess with your mind and make you think anything less about yourself. Stand up tall, put forth your best image and know you are someone special."

"Thanks Nana. You're right."

"Of course I am!" Nana laughed and gave Cassie a big hug.

The following Monday morning, Cassie came downstairs much earlier than usual. She was wearing blue jeans a white tank top.

"Ready?" her mom asked.

"Yep, let's go spend all your money on new clothes just for me," Cassie laughed.

Prayer: Dear Heavenly Father, Please help me realize I am made the way I am because that is how you wanted me. Help me learn to love the body I have instead of finding fault with it. Help me care about what You think, not what other kids think. Thank You for the body you gave me and for making me just as I am.
　　　~Amen

Leaving Behind the Old

Bible Verse: "You have taken off your old self with its practices and have put on the new self, which is being renewed in the knowledge in the image of its Creator." Colossians 3:9-10

Something to Think About: Two years ago, Max was well known in his Middle School. He was the class clown and was always in trouble. When a substitute teacher came to class, she was always warned of Max and his behavior.

Max never worked in class, opting instead to draw inappropriate pictures, talk to his neighbors, and throw paper airplanes he made. He had the worst reputation with the teachers and some students. Other students, however, loved his interruptions and encouraged his behavior.

Over the summer before starting his freshman year of high school, his parents forced him to go to church camp. They didn't think it would help, but sent him anyway just to have a two week vacation from his temper and trouble making.

While Max was at camp, he learned about how God expected him to behave. During those two weeks, he studied more than he was asked and talked to God during his morning devotion time. His whole attitude changed and he gave his heart to God.

When he returned home, his parents were amazed at his transformation, yet they daily held their breath waiting on the old Max to reappear. It never did. God had changed his life permanently.

On the first day of school, his teachers were extra strict and hateful with him. They had heard about his reputation and been warned about what to expect. They were determined to curb him as much as possible. His friends kept talking during class, trying to get him started, but Ma sat quietly, ignoring them. When Alex, his best friend last year, threw paper airplanes at him expecting Max to throw them back, he was shocked when Max picked them up and threw them away.

After six weeks, his old friends began making fun of him. They called him "brainiac" because he was studying and making high marks. They also called him "TP" short for teacher's pet because he had won the teachers' respect. One old friend knew Max was a fighter so he tried starting a fight after gym class. Max just walked away.

As his old friends turned on him, Max began questioning who he was. Although he was happier now, he sometimes felt like he wasn't himself. He didn't know what to do.

When he could take no more, he went to the youth pastor at his church and explained his dilemma. Pastor Rick explained that it was normal to experience this feeling because he had changed. He also explained that it was normal for him to question his self worth now that he was different. Before, his self confidence came from his friends' encouragement and laughter when he acted up. He no longer received that and felt lost. Pastor Rick told him something that truly was an encouragement.

"Max, you have left your old self behind and have made a fresh new start in the eyes of God. You are no longer who others want you to be, but you are now who God wants you to be. That's what's important."

"Yeah, that makes sense," Max replied, "So I guess I just need to make new friends."

"That's a great plan!"

Sometimes becoming a Christian and giving your life to God requires little changes, but often, it means making drastic changes in you than can cause you to be confused. It's okay to feel that way. In fact, it's normal. Just keep in mind that being a different person isn't always bad. You have to become the person God wants you to, not what others want or expect. Follow God and you will be alright!

Prayer: Dear Heavenly Father, Help me and teach me to put my old self behind and start living the life you want me to live. Help the new me, the one who loves and honors You, become strong and renewed.
~Amen

Unseen Beauty

Bible Verse: So we fix our eyes not on what is seen, but on what is unseen. For what is seen is temporary, but what is unseen is eternal. 2 Corinthians 4:18

Something to Think About: Yvonne was a beautiful young girl with long, dark hair, piercing brown eyes and ruby red lips. Everyone commented on her beauty and encouraged her to be a model. She was the envy of all the girls and the dream of all guys. All that changed quickly on a warm summer afternoon.

She had been to the beach with her friends and was riding home in the back seat of Jamie's car. The girls were laughing about the waves knocking them down, discussing the gorgeous life guards with their deep brown tans and singing loudly to the radio. The top was down on the convertible and Yvonne's luscious hair blew wildly in the wind.

As they were crossing an intersection, a large tractor trailer did not slow down and stop for the red light. As he flew threw the intersection, Yvonne and her friends were gliding through it. The truck hit them full force on the passenger side. Her friends suffered mild abrasions and one broken leg, but Yvonne wasn't so fortunate.

The truck hit mostly on her side and left her face severely shattered. Her nose was broken in three places, her chin cruelly removed and pieces of the rocks the truck was carrying destroyed her beautiful eyes.

After many surgeries to replace broken and missing bones and several skin grafts, Yvonne was left with scars that would never heal. Her face was smashed and the scars simply reinforced the mess she was left with. The scar from the laceration on her head was too severe for hair growth, so she was left with a small, but obvious bald spot on the left side of her head.

She was stared at now for her deformities instead of her beauty. It would have been normal for Yvonne to withdraw into a deep depression after loosing her looks. Although she had moments of weakness and found herself crying and angry, Yvonne handled the disfigurement with grace. She knew that although her face looked different, she was still the same person, only stronger.

Yvonne realized that it was God's grace that kept her alive. She hung onto that and gave Him thanks, even on the toughest, most painful days. She did not dwell on the fact she could no longer wear makeup or that kids stared at her, but embraced God's healing power and His blessings.

Once she healed, she began teaching classes on self esteem and self awareness. She encouraged children and teens to find their worth based on who they are, not what they look like.

The beauty people see on the outside is only temporary. An accident, aging, or just someone else's views can change outside looks quickly. What's on the inside is what matters. Having a warm, caring heart, loving others and God, helping those in need, being patient and kind, being a good friend, and never giving up are qualities that will last forever.

Prayer: Dear Heavenly Father, Thank You for the beauty I have on the inside; the beauty that lasts forever. It doesn't matter if my nose is too big or too small or if I think my ears stick out. What matters is who I am. Guide me to be the best me I can be. Thank You.
~Amen

What is Love?

What Is Love Anyway?

What is love? People have tried to answer that question for centuries. It's hard to explain. Go ahead, try for yourself. Explain what love is. Can't do it can you? Don't feel bad, even the best, most educated scholars can't.

There are many different kinds of love. There is the love you feel for your boyfriend or girlfriend. Then, there is the love you feel for your parents and grandparents. You feel an even different kind of love for your siblings and a different kind for friends. You feel love for other church members, your youth pastor, some of your teachers and even strangers.

With so many different kinds of love, is there a right way and a wrong way to love someone? Jesus says yes there is. This chapter takes a look at 1 Corinthians chapter 13 verses 4-6, in which Jesus tells us in detail how love should be. These guidelines, or laws, work for any type of love, even love for your pets.

As you read through this section, think of people you love. Think about how you love them and analyze that love and see if you are meeting Jesus' requirements. If you are – good job. If you aren't, take notes and really think about what you can do different, pray about it and make the changes. You can learn to love with all your heart, just the way Jesus does.

Love is Patient

Bible Verse: Love is patient… 1 Corinthians 13:4

Something to Think About: James and Linda started dating two months ago. They were crazy about one another and madly in love. Last weekend, they went on their third un-chaperoned date. They went to the lake, spread out a blanket and laid down, looking at the twinkling stars in the vast sky. To Linda, it felt like a romantic movie scene and she ecstatic. Linda didn't mind James kissing her; in fact, she had looked forward to it. Her hormones were raging; she was in love and truly enjoyed the shared intimacy. When James put his hand under her shirt, unfastened her bra and reached around the front, she felt uncomfortable, but allowed it. As he kissed her deeper and told her how much he loved her, Linda began giving into the passion. When he suggested they "go all the way", she sternly objected. James got angry.

"Linda, if you really loved me like you say you do, you would do it." he insisted.

"I don't want to. I want to wait 'til I'm married. You know that." she explained.

"Come on Linda. Everyone does it. It isn't a big deal. Why are you being such a baby?" he sighed.

"No, James. Everyone doesn't do it. Even if they are, it's still wrong. And besides, if you really loved me you wouldn't ask me to do something I am not ready for and something I am morally against. You either accept I will not do this until I am married and you never push me again or we are over!" Linda told him.

James was furious. He packed up their things and drove her home in silence. She didn't expect to see him again.

Monday at school, he still wasn't speaking to her, but left a note for her taped on her locker. She hesitantly opened it and read, "I will be at your house at five. We need to talk. –James." She assumed he was coming to break up with her.

When he arrived he looked sad and acted indifferent toward her. He spoke pleasantly to her mom, but didn't joke with her as he usually does. Linda was prepared for the break up.

"Linda, we need to talk." He said as they sat on the front porch swing, looking out over the fish pond.

"I know." She said sadly.

"Look, this is hard on me, but I have to say something." James was obviously nervous and looked down at his shaking hands. After a very long minute, he looked up at her, right into her right blue eyes that were misting with tears.

"I owe you an apology. I am so sorry. After our date, I was so angry and I went home sulking. I was miserable, but I wasn't angry at you. I was angry at myself. You are right, if I loved you, I mean really loved you, I wouldn't want you to do something against your beliefs. And truthfully, if I really loved myself and really loved God, I wouldn't want to go against God either. I prayed for forgiveness and God has forgiven me. Now I ask you to please forgive me as well." James began crying.

"Thank you and I accept your apology. Let's forget it ever happened and move on ok?" she lovingly said.

Three years later, James and Linda were married in a beautiful church ceremony decorated with a vast array of fresh flowers, surrounded by family and friends. That night was the first time they gave into their love in a physical way.

Love is patient. It means being patient in every situation, not just the ones regarding sex. If your brother is being immature and picking on you in front of your boyfriend, you must be patient. He will one day grow up to be your best friend. If you mother wants you to wait to drive, be patient. Ask God to help you with your patience as you grow on your Christian journey!

Prayer: Dear Heavenly Father, Please forgive me for the times I am not patient. Sometimes I just want things to happen when I want them to and have no consideration of others. I ask you to please help me grow in You and learn to wait. I know you are patient with me and don't get angry when I do something wrong, but wait until I learn my lessons and grow. Help me treat others the same way. Thank You.
~Amen

Love is Kind

Bible Verse: …love is kind… 1 Corinthians 13:4

Something to Think About: Miranda was the new girl in school. If that weren't enough, a bad accident when she was young left her with a large scar on her right cheek. Since her father was in the military they moved at least every two years and she seldom made friends. Everywhere she went the students seemed afraid of her, so she learned early to remain alone and ignore them. Walking through the hallways at Oak Hill High School, she felt the stares of other kids. She knew they were trying to figure out what happened to her. Most were avoiding her glare, but some of the brave ones openly stared and many even laughed.

Emily was a Christian. She knew looks weren't what mattered; it was on the inside that counted.

During lunch, Miranda was sitting alone. It didn't bother her, she was used to it. Suddenly, a beautiful red headed girl with the most stunning green eyes sat down beside her. Miranda was prepared for the intense questions and the judgment she would be receiving shortly. This had happened so many times before. Someone, usually the most popular girl, was brazen enough to come and find out the info on her and then relate it back to her friends as they looked over at Miranda and laughed. It was horrible, but she was so accustomed to it, she barely paid it any attention.

"Hey. My name is Emily. You must be the new girl. Welcome to Oak Hill High. I can show you around and help you get acquainted with the school and the teachers if you like. Maybe we can even go out sometimes and I can show you around town. It's small, but it's nice. Our Dairy Dip has the best ice cream of anywhere." Emily said with a big, friendly smile.

"I'm Miranda. That's ok. You don't have to be nice to me. I was in a fire when I was little, that's what's wrong with my face." Miranda said without feeling.

"Oh, well, if you want to talk about it, I am a good listener, but I really just wanted to say hi. We have a great youth group at church if you wanna come with me Wednesday night." Miranda said. It never occurred to her to wander what had happened to Miranda's face. She didn't even notice the scars until Miranda mentioned them, but she had seen her eyes were filled with loneliness and fear.

"Whatever," Miranda said.

From that day on, Emily sat with Miranda at lunch and just talked. She spoke with her in the hallway and always asked her about touring their small town. Emily did not give up. She knew Miranda needed a friend.

Little by little, Miranda came around and the two girls became friends. Emily was right. The ice cream at Dairy Dip was the best and the youth group was awesome. She totally fit in and never felt like anyone was laughing at her. Miranda couldn't believe she had such luck as finding such a true and real friend.

Are you more like Miranda and afraid to take a chance on someone and refuse their hospitality and make friends? Or are you more like the "other kids" who sit back and wonder or laugh at others who are different? If you are, remember, "love is kind". God doesn't ask us to be kind to the ones that are most like us or who are beautiful or popular. He doesn't tell us to be kind only to people we already know. He expects us to be kind to everyone. You can be more like Emily. All you have to do is ask God for guidance and work on being kind. So go out and make new friends, do nice things for people, even strangers. Be the best you that you can possibly be.

Prayer: Dear Heavenly Father, Forgive me for the times when I am not kind. Sometimes I am selfish and forget the feelings of others. Please guide me to do what is right and remind me to be kind to everyone. I want to follow the example Jesus gave and live my life the best I can.
~Amen

Love Does Not Envy

Bible Verse: …{love} does not envy… 1 Corinthians 13:4

Something to Think About: Cousins Ryan and Jacob love playing together, even though they are three years apart. Jacob is now thirteen and Ryan is ten. Often with this age difference, kids don't have much in common, but that isn't the case with these two rambunctious boys. They do everything together, good and bad.

Ryan's mom, Ava, bought him a brand new, shiny metallic blue bicycle. Jacob's bike was old and rust was starting to show. Jacob had been begging for a new bike for months and felt a little sad when Ryan pulled into his driveway on his brand new one. Even though Jacob was sad and wanted a new bike badly, even needed one because his was too small, he wasn't disappointed for Ryan.

"Hey Ryan, that's a really cool bike." Jacob told Ryan.

"Thanks. Mom just bought it for me today." Ryan said enthusiastically.

"May I ride it?" Jacob asked.

"Nah, not now. I just got it and I haven't ridden it much yet." Ryan said triumphantly.

"Oh ok. Well, let me get my bike and let's go for a ride. It really is a great bike Ryan. I am so happy for you." Jacob said, and he meant it.

When someone gets something you want, it's hard to be happy for them. It is sometimes easier to be angry and jealous. Jacob could have easily been mad because Ryan got a new bike, especially when Ryan wouldn't let him ride it. But he didn't. He was happy for Ryan. That's the way you should be. Put yourself in the other person's shoes and think how you would feel. Even when you feel let down, disappointed and sad for yourself, don't blame the other person for getting what you want. Instead, be happy for them.

Jesus was human and He wanted to live. He didn't want to die on the cross. It was painful and humiliating. Yet He did it. He did it for you. And you know what? He is so happy that our sins are forgiven and we can have a relationship with God. He doesn't even resent us because He had to die for us; He is happy for us.

Prayer: Dear Heavenly Father, Please help me not be envious when someone gets what I want or gets something better than what I have. Help me remember to be thankful for all I have and be thankful for what my friends have. Even when I am disappointed, help me always be happy for them instead of being angry.
~Amen

Love Does Not Boast and is Not Proud

Bible Verse: …{love} does not boast, it is not proud. 1 Corinthians 13:4

Something to Think About: Donte is the star basketball player on his school's team. During the last game, he scored the winning goal and broke the school's record for most points earned in a game. He was extremely happy and excited, especially with his friends and family surrounding him, picking him up and carrying him around the court like a king. Pride swelled inside him and he knew he was awesome.

Monday at school, he noticed a huge banner hung in the hallway. It said, "Way to Go Donte!" Cheers and high fives greeted him as he walked down the hall to class. Kids he had never even talked to were walking with him and talking to him. Even his crush, Kiera, was walking with him as she batted her big brown eyes at him. He couldn't believe how great it felt to be a hero.

Later in the week as he was leaving math class for science, he told his long time friend, David, to get his books and carry them for him. David couldn't believe the nerve Donte had and told him no.

"What do you mean 'no'?" Donte asked him. Stars don't carry their own books you twit!" Donte said hatefully.

"You may be a star, but you are still Donte. Stop acting like a snob and get back to being you." David said as he walked off.

Donte was angry. He couldn't figure out why David was acting like this. As he thought about it, he realized a few of his other friends were totally avoiding him. The night before when he called to see if Alex wanted to come shoot some hoops, Alex told him he wasn't in Donte's league and thought he would pass.

At lunch, Donte didn't sit the jocks and popular crowd as he had been, but went to sit with his real friends. One by one, they got up and walked away without saying a word to Donte.

As he went to bed that night, he prayed. "Dear Lord, what have I done? Everyone is mad at me. It isn't fair. It isn't my fault I won the game and broke the record. It isn't fair they are jealous and can't be my friend anymore."

The next morning when he woke up, he had a realization.

"Wow, I know what's wrong. I have been acting like I am better than them and all I have talked about all week is how great I am. No wonder they are mad at me." He went to school and spoke with each of his friends personally and apologized. At lunch, he was back to his regular table and the popular kids who had been idolizing him acted as if he didn't even exist.

"Thankfully, I am myself again and back to normal. Life is good," He said to himself.

You will have things in your life that you have done that are outstanding. There is nothing wrong with celebrating and sharing your accomplishments. Just don't let it consume you and change who you are. Make sure you are just sharing good news, not bragging or making others feel bad. Do not look down on anyone else or expect them to look up to you. Just be yourself.

Prayer: Dear Heavenly Father, Please be with me as I achieve goals in my life. Help me as I make my way through and guide me to the right decisions. When I do something well, please help me keep it in perspective and remember I didn't do it without You. Help me not to brag. I don't want to hurt my friends by acting better than they are. Please watch over me and help me act in ways that honor and glorify You.
    ~Amen

Love is Not Rude

Bible Verse: {love} is not rude… 1 Corinthians 13:5

Something to Think About: Dana talks…a lot! She talks about the weather, animals, her friends, her teachers, her family, TV shows, well, she talks about everything and everyone. LouAnne is Dana's best friend and she likes to talk too, but mostly just ends up listening to Dana.

LouAnne came home from school one evening and her parents were waiting on her. She knew it was bad news. They sat her down and explained they were getting a divorce. LouAnne was extremely upset and called Dana immediately.

"Hello?" came Dana's voice through the phone. LouAnne breathed a sign of relief. She needed a friend right now.

"Hey Dana. It's me. I need to talk. Mom and Dad just told me they are getting a divorce!" Dana cried.

"Oh no. LouAnne, I am so sorry. I remember when my mom and dad divorced. It was just horrible. I cried every night for three weeks. Daddy moved out, but then he got a really cool apartment that had a pool I could go to in the summer so I was OK. And Mom started dating again. That was weird. Oh, the best part was when I went with Daddy because he always took me out for pizza. But yeah, it was tough when they separated. I didn't know how to handle it and I couldn't figure it all out…" Dana went on and on. She never gave LouAnne a chance to speak.

LouAnne was hurting and needed a friend, but Dana was rude and only thought of herself. Instead of LouAnne feeling better after their talk, she felt much worse. She felt her whole world was falling apart and she was lonely. Dana should have listened to what LouAnne was saying and let her cry, but instead, she was self-centered and concentrated on her own life, leaving LouAnne out completely.

The Bible tells us in simple terms, "love is not rude", but that isn't always followed. The next time you are in Dana's situation, stop and think about what the other person needs are before you start babbling like a brook. Putting the other person first isn't always easy, but it can be accomplished. Your parents or grandparents have probably told you at one time or another "put yourself in their shoes". What that means is to think like them. Imagine yourself in their circumstances. What would you need? Would you need someone to listen or someone to chitter chatter and not care about your problems? Of course you would need a friendly ear to hear what you are saying. Everyone needs that during difficult times. So before you catch yourself being rude, stop and think!

Prayer: Dear Heavenly Father, I am so sorry for the times my behavior is rude and I put myself before others. I know that is wrong and I ask you to please forgive me and help me remember to do better. Help me always put others before me and to be helpful when they need me most instead of crushing their spirits. Help me learn to be controlled and be a good friend.
    ~Amen

Love is Not Self-Seeking

Bible Verse: {love}…is not self-seeking… 1 Corinthians 13:5

Something to Think About: A group of four girls, Rebecca, Kirsten, Monique and Shanequa worked hard on a project for school. Rebecca researched the topic thoroughly. Kirsten sorted all the information into categories and Shanequa put everything together for the final product. Monique was elected to be the presenter.

Monday morning in English class, the girls' time had at last came. Monique did a wonderful job presenting the topic, complete with graphs that Kirsten had made, pictures and handouts that Rebecca and Shanequa worked on and background music her brother added for them. She spoke eloquently and clearly. All the girls were thrilled when their project received an A+.

Throughout the day friends and classmates congratulated Monique on a great job presenting. Her teachers were amazed by the professionalism she showed and spoke with one another about it. Monique did not know how to do research or even where to start. She had not clue what category to put the information in and knew nothing about charts or hand-outs. When Shanequa put together the final project and asked Monique for advice, she replied, "I honestly have no clue"; however, she took all the credit. The other three girls were very hurt but said nothing.

Monique was self-seeking. She did not take into consideration the other three girls, but instead acted as if she had done the complete project herself, just so she could receive the accolades and applause.

Have you ever taken all the credit for work others helped you with? If so, you have now heard God's instructions on selfless love and you can change. Next time you are tempted to take the credit, remember this verse and think about Jesus standing right beside you, knowing what you are doing. Think before you act. Always give others credit when credit is due.

Prayer: Dear Heavenly Father, Please forgive me for the times I am led astray and forget to be selfless. Forgive me when I don't give others the credit and praise they deserve. Help me think before I act and live according to Your word. I know all things I do are through You and I want my actions to show that.
    ~Amen

Love is not Easily Angered

Bible Verse: {love} is not easily angered. 1 Corinthians 13:5

Something to Think About: Jose was so excited to go on the school trip to France. He had been waiting all year for the time to come. His sister, Juanita, had heard all the plans he had made and was anxious to hear about his trip. As Jose boarded the plane with his friends, Juanita made him promise to call as soon as he arrived. Neither of them had been on a plane before and she couldn't wait to hear all about it.

After landing in Paris, Jose was busy. His chaperones had a non-stop sight seeing trip planned. He barely had time to take his things to his room before it was time to begin. He thought of Juanita a lot and while he was sitting on the bus riding from site to site he kept a detailed journal just for her.

Juanita waited all day and all evening for Jose to call. With each passing hour, she grew angrier and angrier. She didn't understand how Jose was too busy to call his only sister. Instead of being happy he was having fun or even worrying about his safety, Juanita was mad he hadn't made time to call her.

The Bible verse says love isn't easily angered. This is hard to do, especially in families, but it needs to be done. Instead of getting angry at Jose, Juanita should have put his feelings first and realized he was busy and was out with his friends. It was not an assault on her, but his schedule was jam packed. Next time you feel yourself getting angry over something little, think about it before you explode. Is it really a big deal? Sometimes people do things and you have a right to be angry, but often it is simply a misunderstanding. Maybe you are really stressed out over a big project or test at school and your brother picks on you about something innocent. Normally you just laugh, but today you lash out and yell at him. In that case, you were quick to anger.

Everyone gets angry over stupid things and at times, everyone gets angry quickly. That is normal, but you need to try to avoid that. When you catch yourself getting upset, take a break, pray and think about it. If you have already said something wrong to the other person, go apologize immediately! You can change and become more patient and less angry with God's help.

Prayer: Dear Heavenly Father, Please forgive me when I become angry too quickly or over stupid things. I know this is not how You want me to be and I want to change. Help me learn to be patient, quick to offer forgiveness and slow to become angry.
 ~Amen

Love Keeps No Record of Right or Wrong

Bible Verse: {love} ...keeps no records of wrongs. 1 Corinthians 13:5

Something to Think About: On a cool autumn evening, Margo and Sara were walking along the beach talking. The subject turned to boys, as it often did with the two teens.

"Guess what?" Margo asked.

"What?" Sara replied.

"I am going to ask Ricardo to go to the movies with my brother and me this weekend." She was so excited and couldn't wait. Sara, however, felt differently.

"What do you mean? You know I like Ricardo! You always do this to me. You knew I liked John so you asked him if you could sit with him at lunch. You knew I wanted those cute pink sandals so you had your mom go by them for you. You knew I wanted to be on the yearbook staff at school so you joined first. Even when we were in kindergarten and had to draw a unique picture you drew a sailboat even though you knew that was all I could draw. You are so unfair!" Sara shouted.

Although Sara had a right to be upset with Margo for asking out the guy she liked, she shouldn't have been so angry and she certainly shouldn't have brought up things Margo had done in the past.

Jesus does not do this to us and we should follow his example. When you ask forgiveness, Jesus doesn't say, "Oh and remember last week when you… and the month before when you… and last year when you…?" No, he forgets things we have done in the past. He wipes our slates clean. They are gone and forgotten. You are to do the same thing with family, friends and acquaintances. Let the past remain in the past. Next time you are tempted to bring up old problems, remember Jesus doesn't hold your past against you, so don't hold other's past against them.

Prayer: Dear Heavenly Father, Please help me learn to leave the past alone and not keep remembering it or bringing it up during arguments. Help me forget things others have done to me, just as You forget the things I have done. I know you erase my past and I ask You to teach me to do the same.
~Amen

Love Does Not Delight in Evil

Bible Verse: Love does not delight in evil… 1 Corinthians 13:6

Something to Think About: Her sophomore year of high school, Bailey found out she was pregnant. She hid it for the first seven months with baggy clothes and laughed about eating too much pizza. As her bump grew larger, her friends began asking questions. After awhile, Bailey knew she couldn't hide anymore. It was too much pressure.

"Bailey, what's up with you girl? You aren't eating that much and your belly is huge." Allie asked her.

"Yeah, I agree with Allie. Are you pregnant?" Her friend Christy asked.

"Um, well, promise you will keep it a secret? School is almost out and I don't want anyone to know." Bailey said.

"Of course, we are your best friends. You know you can trust us." The two girls said in unison.

"Well, yeah, I am about seven months pregnant. I will have the baby over the summer and I am giving it up for adoption. Mom and I agree this is the best for the baby. It's really hard and I want to keep her, but I know I am not ready to be a mother. I love her and I just want what is best for her," Bailey admitted.

Her two best friends were very supportive. Bailey felt relieved after sharing the news and felt as if a weight had been lifted from her. With them by her side, she knew she could make it through.

Walking to History class, she saw several students whispering to one another and giggling. She told herself they weren't talking about her and ignored them. Further down the hallway, a guy and girl were talking to one another and lost in their conversation. When she walked by, they stopped talking and looked at her. They guy yelled, "Hey Mama!"

Bailey's friends were all rejoicing in evil. They loved hearing Bailey, the good little girl, being the brunt of the joke and the center of rumors. They loved seeing the perfect, well-behaved Christian girl being brought down.

Their behavior was obviously wrong. Instead of rejoicing in evil and taunting and teasing her, they should have been her friend. She needed support and love instead of malice.

It's easy to give into rejoicing in evil, even in little things, such as being secretly glad when your straight A friend fails a test you passed, or in big things, such as a classmates pregnancy. But we are told this is wrong. Instead of delighting in evil, we need to delight in the good. Befriend those who are in need or who are hurting instead of bringing them down. Instead of joining in the taunting, speak politely to the person and pray for them. Offer encouragement through hard times. You can overcome rejoicing in evil!

Prayer: Dear Heavenly Father, Please help me hate evil instead of rejoicing in it. When I am tempted to rejoice in someone's problems, help me pray for them and offer them help and friendship. Teach me the responsible, Christian way to act, so I glorify You, not my friends.
~Amen

Love Rejoices with Truth

Bible Verse: {love} rejoices with the truth. 1 Corinthians 13:6

Something to Think About: Ruben and April began dating in the summer and had a great relationship. They often went to the movies or for hikes in the mountains. Ruben always made April laugh and she made him feel like the greatest guy ever.

When school started that fall, things began changing. April was in the chorus and often had after school practice, then homework, which took away from her time with Ruben. She also liked to hang out with her friends on Friday nights, but always reserved Saturday for Ruben. Her family was close, so on Sunday's she spent the day with them.

At first, the two began having mild verbal arguments, but by October the arguments escalated. He called her horrible names, told her she was fat, ugly and stupid. April felt sorry for Ruben because his mom left when he was a little boy and he was raised by an alcoholic father. She believed she just couldn't break up with him and desert him as his mother had. Besides, she loved him.

Shortly before Thanksgiving, the fighting got worse and April knew she had to end it. When she told him, he became irate with her. The abuse became physical. He always hit her on the head, back or thighs so the bruises and cuts were hidden. He also threatened to kill himself is she left him; he just couldn't live without her.

During Christmas break, April went to stay a week with her cousin, Whitney. During an emotional evening, April broke down and told Whitney everything but made her promise not to tell anyone. Whitney promised.

After April went back home, Whitney worried constantly. She couldn't sleep and couldn't eat. Her grades were falling and she couldn't concentrate on anything. She knew she couldn't handle this alone and knew she had to protect April.

Whitney told her mom she would like to go visit April and her mother, Tammy. They drove four hours through the country roads to reach their home.

When they went in, Whitney was terrified. She didn't know what to say and she didn't want April mad at her; however, she couldn't bury her head in the sand and pretend nothing was happening.

She silently prayed for God to help her and give her strength to do the right thing.

"Hey, Whitney and April, we just bought that new chick flick you girls wanted to see. Why don't ya'll go upstairs and watch it?" Tammy asked them.

"Actually, Aunt Tammy, I would like to talk to you, Mom and Whitney for awhile if it's ok." Whitney told her.

"Of course! What's on your mind?" April's mom asked.

After Whitney had finished, April stood up, gave her a big hug and said "Thank you!" April showed her mom the hidden bruises and told her how bad things had become. Together the four of them worked out a plan, removed April from the relationship and danger and April and her family began going to church. April started a group at school for girls of date abuse and throughout the next two years helped many of them avoid or get out of abusive relationships.

Whitney did the right thing. The truth could not be hidden. Instead of April being mad at her for telling, she rejoiced the truth had been told and she no longer had to hide.

When you are facing a dangerous situation or even an unethical one, always let the truth shine. There is power, forgiveness and healing in truth.

Prayer: Dear Heavenly Father, Help me always search for the truth and help me do the right things, no matter what the cost.
 ~Amen

Love Protects, Trusts, Hopes and Perseveres

Bible Verse: {Love} always protects, always trusts, always perseveres. 1 Corinthians 13:6

Something to Think About: Anastasia was eight years old the first time her dad's friend, Bill, molested her. She wanted to tell her parents, but his threatening words, "if you tell I will hurt you" kept ringing in her ears. For the next three years, he came to town three or four times a year and stayed with them, always sneaking into her room at night. Anastasia hated when he came to visit and tried to stay with friends. She could usually get away for a night or two, but never the entire visit.

The last night he came into her room, Anastasia hid in her locked bathroom, refusing to come out. Bill banged on the door, yelling for her to get out there and come to him. He said "Ah, come on baby, you know you love it" just as Anastasia's father walked in. Her dad was livid. Instead of cursing him or hurting him, he asked Bill to meet him downstairs. Anastasia's mom called the police and stayed with her and her dad went down stairs with Bill.

A few months later, Anastasia and her family were having dinner when her dad announced he had seen Bill. Anastasia was shocked. How could he visit the monster? Her mom did not appear surprised and simply asked how Bill was doing.

"Dad, how can you visit him after what he has done?" Anastasia asked.

"Because, baby girl, I love Bill." He answered.

"You love him? How can you love him? I hate him and I hope he rots!" She cried.

"Baby, I hope he's in jail for a very long time, hopefully the rest of his life. But he is still a person, a child of God and I can't turn away. He needs to know God's word and I want to give it to him. I took him a Bible and a prayer journal. I know you are mad and you have every right to be. I am mad too. But hate what he did, don't hate him. Pray for him," Her dad explained.

In bed that night, Anastasia thought about what her dad had said. She read the Bible many times and knew she was to love her enemies. She asked God to help her heart be giving instead of stone. It took time, but Anastasia learned not to hate Bill, but hate his ways and actions. She learned to forgive him, not trust him. And she learned to pray for him.

In times like this, it is easy to hate. It seems to come naturally for us; however, God wants us to continue loving. You don't have to hop you ever see someone again or love them enough to spend time with them. Your safety has to come first; but you can hope they find God, find forgiveness and hope their hearts mend and become whole.

Do you have someone in your life you hate right now? Someone who has hurt you and you wish bad things to happen to them? If so give it to the Lord now. Let Him be the judge and jury. Let yourself off the hook. Get away from the bitterness and resentment and forgive them. Pray for them. Pray they find God.

Prayer: Dear Heavenly Father, Please teach me to love instead of hate. Help me learn that to love doesn't mean I have to have a relationship with them, but that I love them enough to want You in their lives. Help me forgive all who have hurt me, just as You have forgiven me. Help me learn to love as You have loved the world.
    ~Amen

PARENTS

Parents!

Parents! They are bossy, demanding, interfering, and don't understand what it's like to be a teen.

Parents are also loving, caring, and helpful, concerned and remember what it was like being a teen. They want to keep you from making the same mistakes they made.

How does God want you to treat your parents? Does He want you to yell at them for reading your journal? Does He want you to slam the door in their face when they tell you not to go out with your friends? How about when you don't do your homework and you get grounded from the phone? Does God even understand how you feel? Does He even care?

God wants you to treat your parents with respect and to honor them by your actions. God instructs parents to raise children by example and discipline, not by being their best friend. Parents want what is best for you, and sometimes that isn't what you want or think you need. Be patient and understanding with them. They probably have a good reason for their actions.

Does God understand and care? Sometimes it doesn't feel like it does it? But He does. He knows your every feeling, thought and concern. He cares deeply about you, but He is your Father and wants to keep you safe and teach you right from wrong. He wants you to be a part of His family. That is why He gave you parents to help you through your younger years.

Obeying your parents isn't easy; in fact, it is often the most difficult thing you have to do. When you feel like blaming your parents and going against their demands remember God gave you to them for a reason. They were the best ones to take care of you and teach you.
Parents aren't perfect, but neither are you. Just as you make mistakes being a kid, they make mistakes being a parent. Try to remember they are doing their best and doing God's will.

When God speaks of parents, He isn't just referring to your biological mother and father. Life gets messed up and complicated and sometimes biological parents aren't in the Picture. If they are, other parents are as well. You may have step-parents, adopted parents, grandparents or foster parents. Your parents may be your aunt or uncle or a friend who is taking care of you. Anyone who is raising you and teaching you how to live is your parent. They all deserve respect and to be honored.

Responsibility and Life Lessons

Bible Verse: Children, obey your parents in everything, for this pleases the Lord. Colossians 3:20

Something to Think About: After a long day at school and what seemed like an even longer bus ride home, the last thing Mandy wanted to do was fold laundry and help cook dinner. Although her mother and father both worked long hours and there were three other children in the house, Mandy didn't think she should have to do anything.

"Mandy, I need your help. Please fold the laundry from the dryer and start a load of towels," her mom requested.

"OK" Mandy stammered.

"Then I need you to help me get dinner started, so please don't dawdle."

"OK!" Mandy half screamed.

After thirty minutes Mandy's mom was ready to start dinner. She called for Mandy but Mandy did not reply. She tried calling her cell phone, but no answer there either. Mandy's mom was getting angry. Finally, Mandy was found sitting outside reading a book under the apple tree.

"What are you doing? Did you do the laundry like I asked?" Mom was irate and hateful.

Mandy nastily answered, "No. It's been a long day and I am tired and needed some time to think."

"You had something to do and you refused to do it. You are grounded for three days!" her mom informed her. Mandy was not happy about this, stomped off to her room and slammed her door. Mom finished the laundry and cooked dinner.

I think all teens go through days like this. Mom or Dad wants you to something and you just don't feel like it. You are tired, have homework to do, want to talk to your friends or maybe just chill out in your room. It doesn't seem fair does it?

Next time you feel like this, consider your parents point of view. Why do they need your help? Perhaps they are over-worked or stressed. You can play an important role in helping them by doing what they ask, or even offer to do more. One thing is for sure; when you help your parents out you are learning responsibility. It isn't an easy or fun lesson to learn, but it is essential and parents know this. You are being prepared to make it your own.

Think about this story. My kids' dad had never washed laundry. His mother always did it for him. When he enlisted in the Army he was eighteen and the men and women in charge of him sure weren't his parents. They expected him to take care of himself, including doing his own laundry. After his dirty clothes all piled up and he had nothing to wear he decided it was time to wash clothes. Going to the laundry mat he had to figure out the laundry detergent, fabric softener and how to work the machines. He managed all that, but he didn't have a clue that he had to sort the colors from the whites. All his white underwear and white Army t-shirts were a pretty pastel pink. Now there is nothing wrong with men wearing pink, in fact I personally love it on men, but the Army, with the macho uniforms, is not the place for pink. Imagine how he felt in the locker rooms in his pretty pink boxers! I know he wished he had learned to do laundry before he joined he left home!

God wants you to help your parents. He wants you to obey them, even when you are tired and cranky. As you become an adult, you will have to go to work, take care of kids and the house as well as many other responsibilities. You don't get a day off just because you don't want to do it. Listen to your parents and obey God's commandment to obey them. You will learn lessons that will carry you through life.

Prayer: Dear Heavenly Father, Please help me on the days when I don't want to listen to my parents. Help me remember Your first commandment, "obey your parents" and do what is right. Help me learn the lessons they are teaching me so I am prepared for adult life.
     ~Amen

Parents Know Best

Bible Verse: Children, obey your parents in the Lord, for this is right. Honor your father and mother – which is the first commandments with a promise – that it may go well with you and that you may enjoy long life on earth. Ephesians 6:1

Something to Think About: Jacob and his friends worked out a plan at lunch. Eric was coming to pick him up around seven and they were headed to the mall. It was Friday night and everyone went out on the weekends. He didn't want to be cooped up with his parents watching another lame movie; he wanted to have fun.

"Dad, I'm going out tonight with Eric, Mike and Sam. I will be home by curfew," Jacob told his dad.

"You aren't going anywhere tonight, Jacob" his dad told him. Jacob was angry at his dad. Everyone else was going out and he would look like a loser; like a little kid without freedom.

"You never let me do anything! You are the worst dad ever! I hate you!" Jacob shouted while stomping out of the kitchen. He slammed the bedroom door when he went in.

Jacob never gave his dad a chance to explain. The snow had begun falling as flurries, but the weather man predicted a blizzard to blow in within an hour or two. Over eight inches of snow was expected by midnight, Jacob's curfew.

His dad was not trying to hurt Jacob nor was he trying to keep him home. He only wanted to keep him safe.

Jacob refused to watch the movie with his parents, but stayed in his room texting his friends. He was so angry. Even as the snow began to pile up over the fence in the backyard, Jacob still thought his dad was stupid, mean and unreasonable. Eric's parents let him go and even let him take the car, and Mike and Sam's parents allowed him to go. It just wasn't fair.

At eleven o'clock the doorbell rang. His parents seldom had company and certainly not at this late hour. His curiosity got the best of him and he went into the living room with his parents. He was surprised to see Mike's parents, Mr. and Mrs. Nelson, in the living room.

As he walked in, Mrs. Nelson asked him if he knew where Mike was. He was supposed to staying at Eric's and they promised since the weather was turning bad they would not go out. Jacob told her he hadn't talked to Mike since the boys left for the mall.

"I called Mrs. James on her cell phone. Apparently the boys lied to both of us. Mr. and Mrs. James are out of town for the evening and trusted Eric to stay at home. He wasn't supposed to have anyone over or go anywhere." Mrs. Nelson told them.

"Oh! That's not what Eric told me. He told me his parents did not care for him having us over and didn't care if he drove us to the mall as long as we were all in by midnight" Jacob admitted.

"I have Mike's mom's phone number. Maybe we should give her a call. What do you think?" Jacob's mom asked.

"I think we should" Jacob's dad agreed.

As they were calling Mike's mom, another knock was heard at the door. Jacob's dad answered, expecting it to be Mike's parents. He figured they were worried as well. He was surprised to see the police asking if Mrs. Nelson was there. They lived in a small town, so it wasn't hard to find anyone.

Detective Daniels and Detective Tolliver came in out of the cold and asked everyone to have a seat. Jacob felt the tears forming against his will as he listened to the detectives telling them about an accident.

"I hate bringing bad news," Detective Tolliver began, "but unfortunately it's a part of our job".

"Eric was driving too fast on a curvy mountain road and he lost control of the vehicle, causing him to spin head on into a salt truck" Detective Daniels stated calmly, but with empathy.

"Oh my gosh, are the boys alright?" Mrs. Nelson asked.

"Well, Eric and Mike are going to be alright. They are at the local hospital in stable condition," Detective Tolliver informed her.

"That's good news. What about Sam? How is he?" Jacob asked through his tears.

"I am really sorry, but Sam has been seriously injured and had to be sent to the medical center sixty eight miles away" Detective Daniels said as comfortingly as he could.

"Have you contacted his parents yet?" Jacob's dad asked.

"No, we were hoping you had their number," Detective Tolliver said.

"Of course, give me just a moment." Jacob's mom said.

As Jacob's mom and the detectives called Sam's parents, Jacob's dad went into the kitchen to call Mr. Nelson. He told him about the accident and volunteered to drive Ms. Nelson to the hospital to meet him.

Jacob suddenly realized the seriousness of the road conditions and didn't want his dad to drive. He begged him not to go.

"Please don't go Dad. Please!" Jacob begged.

"I understand how you feel Jacob, but we have to trust God. If you were in that car, I would do all I could to get to the hospital and I will do the same for Mike's parents. It's the right thing to do" his dad said matter-of-factly.

"Please be careful, Dad!"

"I will, Son".

After they left, Jacob went to his room and prayed, "Dear Lord, thank You for making Dad keep me home tonight and forgive me for getting so angry at him. I know he loves me and wanted to protect me. Please watch over him and Mrs. Nelson as they drive in the storm. Keep them safe. Please be with Sam, Eric and Mike. Help me understand how much Dad loves me and help me learn to listen. Amen."

When you feel your parents don't understand, try to see their side. Jacob thought his dad was being so cruel, when in fact his dad was being responsible and keeping Jacob safe. Parents really do know best.

Prayer: Dear Heavenly Father, please forgive me for the times I don't realize Mom and Dad are trying to help me. Help me learn to see their side and help me learn to appreciate their love and protectiveness instead of being angry about it. Thank you for their love.
~Amen

Giving to Others

Giving to Others

You are helped every day by others. Your parents help you in many ways such as taking care of you, doing your laundry, making sure you are fed and a huge amount of other things. Teachers help by teaching you, many are role models and mentors and some even help with extra curricular activities. Friends help us have fun and have someone to turn to when life stinks. Our pastors and youth pastors help in ways you may not even be aware of. Waitresses, hairdressers, cashiers, police officers, doctors, nurses and so many others are there when we need them. Even our pets help us sometimes. But what do you really give to others?

Sometimes, the answer is a lot, but more often than not the answer is not much.

God tells us we are to be giving to others and to help them. It's easy to give to a friend who needs someone to talk to or to help them with homework, but it is often difficult to help those you don't really like or those you feel don't deserve your help.

This chapter will teach you how to be more giving to others, even those you normally wouldn't give to. Read carefully and with an open mind. You may just find giving to others helps you.

Becoming a Servant

Bible Verse: Your attitude should be the same as that of Christ Jesus: Who being in very nature God, did not consider equality with God something to be grasped, but made himself nothing, taking the very nature of a servant being made in human likeness. And being found in appearance as a man, he humbled himself and became obedient to death—even death on a cross! Phillipians 2:5-8

Something to Think About: Walking down the quiet road near their country home, Trevor and Issac were oblivious to the trash and debris that had been piling up in the ditches. They had grown used to it. Even as they watched a driver throw his fast food restaurant cup and wrappings from the window, they did not pay attention.

As they walked, Jada caught up with them.

"Hey guys, wait up!" she yelled. "Mind if I walk with you?"

The boys both thought Jada was beautiful and secretly had crushes on her, although neither boy would admit it.

"Not at all!" Issac said, hoping she didn't notice his excitement.

They chatted about school, teachers, homework and parents for the next few blocks. Around the corner the trash filled the ditch and was overflowing onto the shoulder of the road.

"Look at this filth. This is gross!" Jada stated with disgust. "I wish someone would do something about this."

"Yeah, like who? The state doesn't care about our road. No one is going to do anything" Issac said.

"Hey, I have an idea. We could do it!" Trevor announced.

"Yeah, right. I'm not cleaning up someone else's trash like a servant," Issac said.

"Come on guys. Why not? I mean, this is our world too. We could make a Saturday of it and get this place looking good again," Trevor said.

"Why bother? By next week people will dump their stuff here again," Jada said sadly. She hated seeing the trash, but agreed with Issac, it wasn't their responsibility.

"So? We do it every weekend then. It's not that big of a deal. It's better than sitting around playing video games. And besides, God wants us to take care of our earth and He wants us to help others. This is doing both." Trevor was getting more and more excited.

"How is that helping others? We are just picking up their trash. That isn't helping them. It will just encourage them to be even more disrespectful and throw more stuff," Issac argued.

"You know, Trevor, you may have a point. We won't be helping those who are throwing it out, but we will be helping our neighbors who live here. They will have a better neighborhood if we clean it up and that's good," Jada said.

The three teamed up and each week they took on the responsibility of cleaning out the ditches. As spring arrived, they planted beautiful wild flowers and grass seed. By May, the neighborhood was luscious and green with multi-colored, vibrant flowers scattered around. The neighbors were all thrilled and each one began doing a little to clean up around their yards.

Jesus tells us to take the role of servant just as He did. He doesn't say, "Hey look, I know some jobs are beneath you so you don't have to worry about doing them." No, He commands we help one another and lose our pride. That's what is important. So start today and do something you always felt was beneath you, whether it's helping a classmate who is struggling with math, carrying the tray for the boy with a broken arm or cleaning up trash around your neighborhood. Become a servant!

Prayer: Dear Heavenly Father, help me realize I am no better than anyone else. Help me learn to be a servant who serves only one master, You. When there is an opportunity for me to help, teach me to lose my pride and dig in and do what needs to be done. Teach me and guide me in Your ways Lord.
    ~Amen

Give Generously

Bible Verse: Give generously to {others} and do so without a grudging heart; then because of this the Lord your God will bless you in all your work and in everything you put your hand to. Deuteronomy 15:10

Something to Think About: On a cold night in January, when a heavy blizzard had hit and eight inches of snow lay on the frozen ground, the wind howled angrily around sixteen year old Michael. Standing outside in just a pair of flannel pajamas he was chilled to the bone. His only pair of shoes and winter coat were inside, being consumed by a raging fire that took all the family had. His parents were away visiting family so Michael stood watching the inferno all alone.

Watching his home and few possessions burn to the ground, Michael did not know what they would do.

His neighbors, Mr. and Mrs. Mitchell ran out of their home when they heard the fire sirens and found Michael watching his home burn as tears ran down his cheeks. Michael had been a difficult kid, often rummaging through the Mitchell's garage and messing things up. He often fought with their only son, Byron. Byron was known as "the brain kid" and made straight A's, was involved with all the scholastic clubs and put school work above everything else. He excelled in everything he did, a direct opposition from Michael, who barely passed his classes and was only involved with the "bad" kids in school. He often cut classes and stood outside smoking instead of learning. Mr. and Mrs. Mitchell wanted nothing to do with Michael; however, upon seeing him standing there alone and cold, their views changed.

Mrs. Mitchell walked up to him. Michael's first reaction was to step away. She was always into his business and yelling at him for cutting through her yard and messing up her precious rose bushes. He didn't feel like a confrontation tonight, of all nights.

"Michael, come home with us. We will give you some of Byron's old clothes and give you the spare room. You are welcome to stay as long as you like," Mrs. Mitchell told him.

Michael went home with them and although Byron's clothes were preppy, whereas he was used to wearing grunge, he was appreciative. His parents decided to stay in Okalahoma, leaving Michael to fend for him self. His dad told him, "When I was your age I was on my own, now you are too. You will be fine. It will make you a man."

The Mitchell's lovingly took him into their family and raised him as their own. Throughout the time he lived there his grades improved, his appearance was less rugged and he learned manners. After going to a community college for two years, he transferred to a four year university, where he graduated with a bachelor's degree and with honors. After graduation, he went on to seminary school and began teaching the Word of God to others. Had the Mitchell's put themselves first and not reached out to Michael, his life would have turned out differently.

When faced with helping someone you do not like, do so without hesitation. Do not resent it, even if the outcome isn't as great as Michael's. Use the example Jesus gave us and give with your heart and soul.

Prayer: Dear Heavenly Father, I come to You today asking You to help me learn to give generously. Help me do it because I want to and do it from my heart. Help me not feel like it is a chore. Help me not hold grudges or expect anything in return. Help me be more like Jesus and do what is right.
~Amen

Giving to the Oppressed

Bible Verse: …if you spend yourselves in behalf of the hungry and satisfy the needs of the oppressed, then your light will rise in the darkness, and your night will become like the noonday. Isaiah 58:10

Something to Think About: Marc sees a homeless bum on the street every day on his way to work at his after school job at the grocery store. Marc judges him as being lazy, ugly and someone to stay away from. Every day Marc sighs in disgust as he sees the dirty man with the mangy beard and long hair. For goodness sake, the man needs a bath. Marc can smell him from the car as the wind carries the old man's foul aroma through the air.

Sunday morning at church, the preacher talks about giving to others. Marc is touched and realizes he does nothing to help others, only him self, and vows to himself and to God that he will change. He just doesn't know where to start.

A month goes by. Marc still stares in disgust at the bum, hating him for his state of being. He still prays God will show him where he can help others, but finds no answers.

Finally, Marc sees clearly and knows he is to help the old bum. Marc asks for a vacation day, but leaves home the same time as usual. He pulls his car into a lot near where the old man stands, parks and hesitantly gets out. Walking over to the man, Marc is nervous, scared and disgusted but he keeps walking.

"Hi!" Marc says to the bum. "I am Marc."

The man just stares at him with vacant eyes.

"There is a café next door. Do you want to go with me to get something to eat? I also have a little money saved up and rented you a motel room. I will let you go there, take a shower and put on fresh clothes I brought you. You can sleep there tonight if ya want" Marc told him.

The man smiles weakly and agrees to go.

During their lunch, the man tells Marc his name is Omar. He was once a highly praised Real Estate Agent in a town nearby and had a lot of money. Marc doesn't believe him.

"So what happened? How did you go from that life to this one?" Marc asks with accusations.

"Well, the market crashed and houses weren't selling. I had all my money sunk up into my own business and little by little it just dwindled away. The day my home foreclosed my wife left and I haven't heard from her since. I had a little money and stayed in motels for two months while trying to find another job. The economy was bad then and I couldn't find anything, not even a job bagging groceries. After awhile, all the money was gone and I had nothing and nowhere to go," the man admits.

"I am so sorry. Well, let's go and you can get cleaned up." Marc tells Omar.

Marc leaves Omar at the hotel and tells him he would be back later to take him to dinner. While Omar showers and naps, Marc goes and speaks with his father. His father is as skeptical as Marc is, but after doing some research on the internet and finding Omar's story checks out, his dad is glad to help.

Marc and his dad, Steve, go to the hotel and pick up Omar and take him out to a buffet dinner, where Omar eats ravishingly. As they eat, Steve tells Omar his plan.

Steve gives Omar five new outfits and two new suits that fit him perfectly. They allow him to stay at the hotel but use Steve and Marc's address as Omar's permanent residence so he can find a job. Within two weeks, Omar finds a job at a real estate agency as an agent selling beach front homes. Within three months, Omar saves enough money to rent a nice home in a respectable neighborhood and is back on his feet.

Marc and Steve fed the hungry. Omar was hungry for food, water and shelter, but he was also hungry for companionship and acceptance.

When you approach a new student at school or a lonely kid at the park and befriend them, you are feeding them friendship. When you offer the construction workers down the road from your house who have been working hard all day in the hot sun a glass of water, you are relieving thirst. Do not leave the oppressed alone, but reach out to them, giving them a helping hand when you are able. You do not have to go to the extreme Marc went, but just handing a homeless person a bacon biscuit and coffee from your car window is a huge step (always have an adult with you when you approach any stranger). Giving someone a smile reaches their heart. Use your heart and soul and see where needs can be met.

Prayer: Dear Heavenly Father, Thank You for providing for me and giving me food, water, shelter and love. Please help me reach out to those who aren't as fortunate as I am. Help me see where I can help and lead me to opportunities. Speak to me when I am tempted to walk away and teach me to do my part, or even more than my share. Help me love the oppressed and lonely and teach me to help them.
 ~Amen

Using Your Gifts

Bible Verse: Each one should use whatever gift he has received to serve others, faithfully administering God's grace in its various forms. 1 Peter 4:10

Something to Think About: Having a singing voice as beautiful as any they had heard, Adrienne was the first one mentioned when the band, "Gators" needed a lead singer. Sam, Tom and Zena talked to Adrienne and tried to convince her to join the group, which meant she would be singing songs about sex, drugs and other immoral things she was against. Adrienne loved singing better than anything and singing with the "Gators" was a step toward fame. She knew she would be singing at some of the nightclubs where talent scouts often visited looking for new talent to sign contracts. As excited as she was, something was holding her back and she told the group she would have to think about it.

Any time Adrienne had an important decision to make, she always prayed first, relying on God to lead her to the right decision. As she went to bed, Adrienne once again prayed, "Dear God, I don't know what to do. I know singing for the group would help me in my career. A talent scout could hear me and I could finally begin to make a living doing what I do best. I know their lyrics aren't always moral, but I can go so far with them. Their last singer just signed a major contract and is now making a great deal of money. I could buy Mom a new car and my brother the guitar he has his eye on. I could really be something special if I can make it with the band. Help me make the right decision. Amen."

The next morning, Adrienne woke up early for church. It was her week to sing the special song of the service and she loved watching everyone's eyes glisten with tears as she sang of God's forgiveness and love. During the service, she was more emotional then usual. Looking out at the congregation and knowing she was making a difference in other's lives through her singing, she realized she was doing the Lord's work. She knew her gift was song and it was a gift from God. As she sang, she made the decision to not join the group and to find a way to sing and glorify God. She wanted to help others find God, not lead them down the road to immorality.

You have many talents and may not even be aware of your gift. Perhaps you are a writer or poet, or have a great singing voice. Maybe you can make a keyboard sing or the drums beat in perfect time. Maybe you are great with kids or have a way with the elderly. No matter what your talent is, it comes from God. Use your gifts to glorify His name and to help and serve others.

Prayer: Dear Heavenly Father, Thank You for the gifts You have granted me. Help me use them to be a servant to others and let Your light be seen through my gift. Help me not use my gift for self gratification but to give to others and show me the best ways to do that.

~Amen

Offering Help to Other Believers

Bible Verse: {Jesus said} "I tell you the truth, anyone who gives you a cup of water in my name because you belong to Christ will certainly not lose his reward." Mark 9:41

Something to Think About: Daisy was at church Sunday morning when she noticed Samantha was sitting in her seat with her head held low. Usually Samantha was the life of the party, but this one morning, she looked distraught instead of bright and sunny. Daisy and Samantha had never been friends since Samantha was five years younger than Daisy, but Daisy knew Samantha had a strong belief and was a great girl.

Walking over to Samantha, Daisy asked her, "Are you alright?"

"Yeah," Samantha answered sadly.

"You sure? You seem really down. If you need to talk I am here and I am a really good listener," Daisy told her.

"Well, Mom told me this morning her and Dad are getting a divorce and I'm just really bummed about it," Samantha admitted.

"I went through that a few years ago with my parents too. I know how you feel. It's really hard to get through it. How 'bout I call you after church and we can talk?" Daisy asked.

"That would be great!" Samantha replied.

Although they had never been friends and barely talked, Daisy reached out to a fellow Christian, Samantha, when she was in need. God tells us when we help other believers our deeds will not be forgotten, but will be rewarded. If you see a fellow believer in need, reach out and help them.

Prayer: Dear Heavenly Father, Please help me remember to reach out to other believers when they need me. Help me not sit back and think they are alright just because they are Christians. Everyone hurts sometimes and we all need help. Teach me to give when others have needs.
    ~Amen

Praying for Others

Bible Verse: As for me, far be it from me that I should sin against the Lord by failing to pray for you. I will teach you the way that is good and right. 1 Samuel 12:23

Something to Think About: Zoe moved to town on a Tuesday. She remembered it was a Tuesday because she met Eve that night, who promptly invited her to church the next night for the youth meeting. Zoe was excited to make a friend but wasn't thrilled about church. She didn't believe in God and thought organized religion was an ancient idea; however, Eve was so nice she accepted the invitation.

Eve felt great about Zoe coming to church with her, but after spending a little time with Zoe, Eve was skeptical. She did not believe as everyone else did and she often used vulgar language. Eve was so upset when Zoe came over to walk to church because of Zoe's clothes. Zoe wore all black, even black nail polish. She was one of the "goth" girls who Eve stayed as far away from as she could.

At church, Zoe felt left out and lonely. Eve and the other kids ignored her and laughed behind her back. It was torture. Once the evening was over, she knew she would not go back to church. Zoe went home feeling more alone and afraid than she had before she came to town. All her hopes and dreams of having friends and fitting in were scattered in the wind.

Eve didn't think much about Zoe. All she thought was "I gotta stay away from her. She's nothing but bad news." Eve never got to know Zoe. She never found out she wore all black because everything else was still packed or that her nails were painted black because her sister, who was fighting cancer, was experimenting with different nail colors and that is the color it happened to turn out. Eve didn't take time to learn that Zoe had never in her life been to church nor had she ever heard much about God, except when someone was cursing Him. All Zoe knew was God was someone to be afraid of and she afraid enough without adding something else. Eve also never found out the reason Zoe, her mother and sister moved to town. Zoe's dad was an alcoholic who had beaten Zoe and her sister since they were three and Zoe's sister was fighting a tough battle with cancer and needed stability, less stress and to live closer to the medical center where she received treatments. All Eve saw was a rough girl to be afraid of.

Even if Zoe was all Eve thought she was and someone to stay away from that doesn't excuse all of Eve's behavior. We are required, by God, to pray for others, especially those who do not know Him. Eve should have prayed consistently for Zoe and been an example to her. Instead, Eve's behavior cemented into Zoe's min more than before that Christians thought they were better than anyone else.

When someone is different than you, take time to get to know them a little and show Christians are caring and loving. Do not write them out of your mind, but instead pray for them. If they are someone you do not need to be associated with because of safety issues, that doesn't let you off the hook. You still have to pray for them. Lift them up to God and let Him do the work.

Prayer: Dear Heavenly Father, Please help me remember to pray for all those who do not know You. Teach me to be an example to them and show them the care and love You have. Please lead me and teach me to be a true Christian and have a caring heart and most of all, Lord, please teach me to always pray for others, lifting them up to You, in Jesus' name.
    ~Amen

Hospitality

Bible Verse: Offer hospitality to one another without grumbling. 1 Peter 4:9

Something to Think About: On his way to school, Zane watched his archenemy, Dyquan, board the bus with his book bag, a poster board and a large cardboard box. Dyquan was having a hard time keeping all of it in his hands, and once in his seat he had no where to sit them. Zane laughed inside at the disaster. Dyquan had picked him for the last four years, calling Zane four-eyes, square peg, goody-goody, and words Zane wouldn't even think. Zane was a Christian while Dyquan was an atheist. Zane was really enjoying watching Dyquan struggle for once and thought, "serves him right".

As Zane watched, he thought about Jesus. If Jesus was here on this bus and Dyquan had taunted Him for years would Jesus sit in his seat laughing on the inside? And if Jesus were in the seat beside Zane, what would He think about the way Zane was reacting?

"Hey Dyquan, I have room in my seat. You can sit some of your things here," Zane told him.

Dyquan looked around for the voice and when he saw it was Zane, he looked started. "Um that's ok. I don't want my stuff torn up," he said hatefully.

"It won't get torn up. Look, I have the room and your things won't get squished. When we get to school I can help you carry them in. Your homeroom is right next to mine. It won't be a problem at all."

Dyquan smiled and said, "Hey thanks. I appreciate it."

Dyquan and Zane never became friends, but Dyquan stopped picking on Zane and even spoke to him from time to time. Zane did not offer to help Dyquan to make himself look better or to hurt Dyquan's things. He did it because God wants us to show kindness to others, even when they haven't been kind to us. Zane did exactly what Jesus asked of him.

Prayer: Dear Heavenly Father, Thank You for the opportunities I have in my life to show hospitality to others. Help me always keep You in mind and help others when I have the opportunity. Teach me to behave as Jesus did and show love and concern for others.

~Amen

Temptation

Temptation

Have you ever been tempted to do something you shouldn't? I already know your answer is "yes." Everyone is tempted. Even Jesus was tempted.

What did you do when you were tempted? Did you give in to the temptation even though you knew it was wrong or did you walk away? I bet at different times you have done both. No one is perfect. Not your parents, your preacher, your friends, or *gasp* teachers. There have been times everyone gives into temptation.

Maybe your mom told you not to eat the last piece of chocolate cake, but it looked so good you couldn't help it. Or perhaps you forgot to study for your math test and during the test you could easily see your friend's paper so you sneaked a small peek to see the answer to number five. Maybe you were at a party and your friends tried to convince you to have a drink and although you didn't really want to, you ended up doing it just because everyone else was.

When you are tempted do you ever feel Jesus doesn't understand? Do you ever feel He just doesn't know what it's like to be a teen these days? Well, he does understand. Having lived as a human, Jesus feels every emotion you have ever felt, understands every temptation you are faced with and knows how difficult it is to resist temptation. He knows how hard life can be and He is there to help you through. Rely on His words of wisdom and His Word and you too can turn from temptation.

Temptation is often difficult to overcome. It is hard to "just say no" and walk away, but remember God's Word and allow Him to help you through these difficult situations. There will be times when you slip, but there will be more and more times you won't. Hang in there and keep on praying.

Jesus Understands

Bible Verse: For we do not have a high priest (Jesus) who is unable to sympathize with our weakness, but we have one who has been tempted in every way, just as we are – yet without sin. Let us then approach the throne of grace with confidence, so that we may receive mercy and find grace to help us in our time of need. Hebrews 4:15-16

Something to Think About: At a party over the weekend, Jalen's friends drank a great amount of beer. Jalen refused. He was having a terrible time sitting around just watching, but was too shy to dance or mingle and make new friends. His best friend, Jared, was shy as well, but after several beers he was out on the dance floor having the time of his life. Jalen was tempted to jump in and join the party, but after watching his uncle suffer and die from alcoholism, he avoided it.

When Jalen went home, he felt terrible. He tried to pray but words wouldn't come. He was angry. Jesus expected so much of him yet Jesus never went through what Jalen went through. He didn't have step-parents and brothers who were so irritating to contend with. He had never been to a party and wanted to fit in but couldn't because of His beliefs. It just wasn't fair.

Jalen fell asleep thinking about how unfair Jesus was. As he slept, he dreamed he was back in time, back when Jesus was a young man walking on the earth as a human. Together the two of them walked into a marketplace. They saw kids gambling, heard cursing and watched as other young men, even a few women, drink and dance and laugh. Everyone looked like they were having so much fun.

"Hey, here comes Jesus, the goody two-shoes of Nazareth!" someone shouted.

"Yeah. Hey Jesus, are you going to the synagogue again?" another jeered.

"Jesus, come have some fun for once. Join us. Have a couple drinks. Get in on the betting, you may even win enough to get your folks out of debt!" another taunted.

Jesus stood firm. "No thanks."

Although they appeared to be having fun and Jalen and Jesus would have enjoyed the party, Jesus knew it was wrong and against his heavenly and earthly fathers' wishes. It was tempting to place a few bets and win enough money to pay everyone. With his special miraculous powers, He knew he could turn the tables and be assured a win, but again, Jesus knew this was wrong.

Jalen felt the temptation Jesus was facing because he was facing it as well. He woke up the next morning understanding Jesus had been tempted. He was tempted by the devil three times and even offered the whole world. He was tempted by his peers and even by women. But Jesus had stood firm.

Waking up, Jalen finally understood. He prayed, "Dear Jesus, I am sorry. I know that You understand and You feel my pain and temptations. Thank You for enlightening me and helping me see clearly. Amen."

Do you sometimes feel Jesus doesn't really understand and that He doesn't care? Don't beat yourself up for that, everyone feels that way from time to time. But do think about it and learn more about the temptations Jesus went through. He really does understand. Learning to resist temptation will help you grow stronger in Jesus and help you be a stronger, more mature Christian. Think before you do something and ask Jesus to guide you.

Prayer: Dear Heavenly Father, Please help me and guide me in my daily life. When I am tempted please help me be strong and do what You would do. I want to do the right things and I want to be a better Christian, but I really need Your help. Thank You.
~Amen

Watch for Temptation

Bible Verse: {Jesus said} "watch and pray so that you will not fall into temptation. The spirit is willing but the body is weak." Matthew 26:41

Something to Think About: Chloe and Savannah were among the unpopular crowd. The two of them sat at lunch watching all the popular kids laughing and kidding and wished they were part of them. They were never invited to parties or asked to go out on dates. It was a lonely time for the girls and they felt worthless.

At the mall on Friday night, Chloe and Savannah saw Mariah and Brooke, the most popular, beautiful girls in school. They couldn't help but eavesdrop on their conversation.

"I want to run in the lingerie store. Do you mind coming with me?" Brooke asked Mariah.

Mariah responded, "Not at all. In fact, I need a new padded push up bra. This one is starting to deflate."

"Yeah, me too. I hope no one we know is there. I would die if anyone knew I wore a padded water bra to make me look two cups larger than my small A cup" Brooke admitted.

"Me too! If I didn't wear a great bra I would be flatter than Chloe" Mariah laughed.

Chloe and Savannah stood in silence, too shocked to even speak. Did they hear right? Did the two girls with the best figures really have to wear padded bras?

"Wow!" Savannah exclaimed. "Chloe we can so tell everyone about this. It's going to be great. They deserve it. It will deflate their big fat obnoxious ego just like it deflates their breast size!" Savannah laughed viciously.

"Yeah, this is gonna be great. Let them see what it's like to be made fun of for a change," Chloe said.

The girls talked for the rest of the evening about getting back at Brooke and Mariah. They couldn't wait. When Chloe went home, she began thinking about how terrible the girls had made her feel over the years. They always made fun of their small breasts and their height. Both girls were shorter than everyone else and it was often the butt of the jokes. She called Savannah to gloat again about how great it was going to be.

"Savannah, I have been thinking about this and I am so excited I can barely wait until tomorrow!" Chloe said.

"Yeah, I have been thinking about it too. Look, I have to admit I am so tempted to do this, but I just can't go through with it. I know this isn't how God wants us to act. It just isn't right!" Savannah said.

"But Savannah, we have to do it. This is our big chance" Chloe begged.

"No, we just can't do it. We have to fight the temptation. You know how they make us feel? We don't want them to feel that way. Ok, maybe we do, but that is wrong. We need to just keep quiet and do the right thing."

"Oh, OK. I guess you are right. Thanks!" Chloe said.

Temptations are everywhere. We are tempted with lying, stealing, gossiping, and telling something we have overheard. We are sexually tempted and tempted to let our homework slide and cheat off a friend. There are so many ways Satan temps. The best way to avoid temptation is to watch for it. Know it is there and know that Satan is going to try his best to try to trip you up. Keep your eyes open and your heart on God. Pray He helps divert temptation from your path.

Prayer: Dear Heavenly Father, I know temptations are a part of life and I know there will be times I am tempted. I pray that you watch over me and help me keep my eyes open and look out for temptation. Help me to avoid it and do the right things. ~Amen

Judgment

Judgment

I can't believe she said that? What was she thinking?" Allie asked Martha.

"I don't know but it was so stupid," replied Martha.

"Yeah, she's just a dumb country girl. She doesn't know anything." Allie sneered.

"Exactly. I mean her parents are drunks and she's gonna be one too. She's never going to be anything but a stupid drunk!" Martha stated.

"I know, right? I hate it when she speaks to me. It's so embarrassing to even know her let alone have her speak to me as if we are friends." Allie said.

Have you ever been the subject of a conversation such as this one or have you ever been a participant in one? Being judged by others hurts a lot. Self-esteem is vanquished and it is difficult not to believe the rumors about yourself or others.

This chapter will help you when you are tempted to judge others as well as help you deal with the pain when someone judges you. Pray as you read this, take notes, whatever you need to do. You can overcome judgment with God's help.

Judge Not

Bible Verse: "Do not judge or you too will be judged. For in the same way you judge others, you will be judged, and with the measure you use, it will be measured to you.

"Why do you look at the speck of sawdust in your brother's eye and pay no attention to the plank in your own eye? How can you say to your brother, 'Let me take the speck out of your eye,' when all the time there is a plank in your own eye?" Luke 6:41

Something to Think About:

"Wow, would you look at how short Marissa's shorts are? I can't believe she is wearing them!" Suzie asked Kendra.

"I know! I wouldn't be caught dead in them," Kendra responded.

"You would think she would look in a mirror and notice wouldn't you? I mean, they are so inappropriate!" Suzie asked.

Although Marissa did not know the girls were talking about her, she still felt self conscious of her shorts. She had a growth spurt over the weekend and her jeans were all too tight and were now high waters. Her shorts seemed to have shrank in length and were all way shorter than she liked. Today was 96 degrees outside and she couldn't bear to wear sweat pants all day, so she wore her longest pair of shorts, which she knew were still too short.

As Marissa was thinking about her shorts, she overheard a conversation in the hallway.

"Hey, can you believe Kendra is wearing a shirt that shows so much cleavage? I mean, it's cut as low as the girls in magazines. She should know better!" Jessie said.

"I don't know, I kinda like it," Jack admitted.

"Jack, you are such a pig!" Jessie told him.

Kendra had been talking about how short Marissa's shorts were and was judging her. It was not Kendra's fault, and she knew how bad they were, but it was her only option. Kendra was judging her, but at the same time, another couple was judging Kendra because of her low cut top. Kendra had been judging someone else on their appearance when she was ignoring her own indiscretion in dress.

We are taught to withhold judgment when we have a plank in our own eye. Of course that doesn't mean a literal plank. It means, who are we to judge others when we aren't perfect ourselves? The only one perfect is Jesus. Next time you are tempted to judge others, remember you are not perfect and have no right to judge anyone else. Leave that for God.

Prayer: Dear Heavenly Father, Thank You for showing me the right way to behave. Please forgive me for the times I slip and judge others. Help me remember we are all imperfect and have our faults. Help me be an encouragement to others and lift them up instead of beating them down. Thank You Dear Lord.
~Amen

Passing Judgment

Bible Verse: You, therefore, have no excuse, you who pass judgment on someone else, for at whatever point you judge others, you are condemning yourself, because you who pass judgment do the same thing.

So when you, a mere man, pass judgment on them and yet do the same thing, do you think you will escape God's judgment? Romans 2:1

Something to Think About: Ted missed church Sunday because he had stayed out too late partying again. It had become a habit and he only attended church once every six weeks or so and only when his mom absolutely made him.

Rebecca and Ted had gone to church together since they were babies. They were dedicated to the Lord at the same time and even share their baptism day. Rebecca loved sharing her faith with him and Ted always had the same views. But things had recently changed.

Last week, Ted invited Rebecca to dinner with him. She said yes and was looking forward to catching up. During mid-term exams they hadn't had much time to chat and she missed him.

During dinner, Ted guzzled three beers. Rebecca tried to discuss it with him, but he didn't want to hear it.

Rebecca made the decision to put a temporary cease in their close friendship, at least until Ted straightened up. She didn't want to be around alcohol and parties and she didn't want temptation to be put in her way. She also didn't want to give up on Ted.

"Look Ted, I know right now we have different values and that's ok, but I just don't think I can hang out with you while you are partying and drinking," she told him.

"It's no big deal Rebecca. Maybe you should loosen up and have a drink. You wouldn't be so frigid then," Ted said.

"Ted, I will always care about you and when you start acting like yourself again, give me a call. I'm not mad at you or anything, but I just can't be friends right now," Rebecca said sadly.

"Whatever," Ted said as he walked off.

Rebecca was sad, but she knew she had done the right thing. Although she strongly disliked Ted's actions and broke off a friendship to protect her own values, she didn't turn against Ted nor did she judge him. She kept taking to him at school and tried to be an example to him.

When you pass judgment onto others you are sinning. This does not mean you should hang out with the wrong crowd. You still have to avoid dangerous situations. It means, however, that you can not be hypocritical in your thinking. You don't have to like what someone is doing, but you can't think they are a bad person because of it. Love them but hate their behavior. Their judgment is in God's hands, not yours.

Prayers: Dear Heavenly Father, it is so easy to fall into the judgment trap and look down on people. Help me remember even though I do not agree with their behavior, they are still Your children and deserve my love and prayer. Help me lift them up to You and help me set an example for them through my own behavior.
~Amen

Slander and Rumors

Bible Verse: …Do not slander one another. Anyone who speaks against her brother or judges him speaks against the law and judges it. When you judge the law, you are not keeping it, but sitting in judgment on it. There is only one Lawgiver and Judge, the One who is able to save and destroy. But you – who are you to judge your neighbor? James 4:11-12

Something to Think About: Slander means to do damage to another person's character. Gossip magazines are full of slander. But there are other ways to slander.

William was at the grocery store with his mom one night and saw his teacher, Ms. Scott. Ms. Scott was the teacher who always assigns homework, even on weekends and holiday breaks, and calls parents when homework isn't turned in. She was buying a bottle of wine. William didn't know who the wine was for, or why she bought it, but he went to the school next day with his story ready. He really wanted to get back at her for making his life miserable.

"Wow, Ms. Scott is extra tough today!" Marc said.

Yesterday the class had been out of control and rude to the substitute teacher and deserved the extra homework and the lunch detention they had received, but Marc and William didn't see this. They only believed she was being mean.

"Yeah!" William responded. "It's because she is hung over."

"What do you mean? How do you know that?" Marc asked curiously.

"Well, Mom and I were at the grocery store last night and she bought a bottle of wine. I just know she went home and drank it all by herself and now she's hung over," William answered with pride.

The truth was, Ms. Scott did buy a bottle of wine. What William didn't know, or bother to find out, was her oldest daughter just received an acceptance letter for medical school and would be starting in the fall. Ms. Scott threw her a small, impromptu congratulations party and a group of eight shared the one bottle of wine. Ms. Scott drank Diet Pepsi.

Even if Ms. Scott had drunk the whole bottle herself, what business would that have been of William's and what business did he have telling everyone? He wouldn't want Ms. Scott to tell everyone that she found him sitting at his desk crying last week because he didn't get the lead part in the school play. It's the same thing.

Think before you speak. Do not spread rumors. Do not tell things that will cause pain or harm to anyone else. As my dad used to tell me, "mind your own business".

Prayer: Dear Heavenly Father, Please open my eyes so that I may see when I hurt others. Help me stop and think before I speak. I don't want to speak badly of anyone and I don't want to hurt them. Keep my heart open and my mouth shut when I am tempted to spread rumors.
~Amen

Judgment from Others

Bible Verse: "I care very little if I am judged by you or by any human court; indeed, I do not even judge myself. My conscience is clear, but that does not make me innocent. It is the Lord who judges me." 1 Corinthians 3-4

Something to Think About: Amberly and her family moved to town one week before school started. She didn't have a chance to meet anyone before she walked through the school doors on the first day.

At lunch on the first day, Wade came and sat with her. He was tall, handsome and very charming. Amberly didn't know that Wade had a reputation as a lady's man and people thought he slept with every girl in school. Had she known, Amberly wouldn't have cared.

Amberly and Wade became good friends and spent a good bit of time together. Through her band and JROTC classes, Amberly also made several other close friends, including Amanda, who wasn't thrilled Amberly was friends with Wade.

"Amberly, honey, do you know what kind of reputation Wade has? He is known as the guy who sleeps with everyone. He isn't someone you should be friends with."

"I don't care what others think. I like Wade and we are just friends," Amberly stated.

"But, you are going to get a reputation just by being his friend." Amanda said with concern.

"Look, I appreciate what you are trying to do, I really do. But, I know what my relationship is with Wade and I have got to know Wade and know who he really is. I don't care what others think. Besides, it is God whose judgment matters to me and I know I am doing nothing wrong, so it's no one else's business."

Amberly knew she was not doing anything against God, in fact, she was doing exactly what God wanted her to do…be someone's friend regardless of what others think. Wade turned out to be a great guy, who was still a virgin, despite what the other kids thought. She didn't let it get her down when others said something negative about her, she lived by her heart.

When someone says something negative about us or tells things that aren't true, it's hard not to care and be hurt. But just remember, God is the only One who can judge you. Live by your heart and do what is right and don't worry about what anyone else thinks.

Prayer: Dear Heavenly Father, Thank You for freeing me from judgment. It does not matter what others think of me, only what You think You are my only judge. Please help me remember this when other judge me and help me overcome it. Thank You.
~Amen

Hope in God

Hope in God

Some days it just feels like your whole world is falling apart. Listening to the news and hearing about deaths, accidents, murders, and the economy is scary. Going to school you see kids who stay in trouble and may see students involved with drugs and/or gangs. Your parents may be divorcing or fighting or your grandparents may be sick. Everywhere you turn there is bad news. It's so easy to get discouraged and lose all hope. But there is always hope!

God will never, ever forsake you or leave you. No matter what is going on in your life or the lives of those you love, God is always on your side. Heartaches and pain will still come but He will see you through it.

Remember, the rain waters the gardens and flowers and when the rain dries up the sun shines brightly once again. Storms come but don't last forever. Winter is cold and dreary, but spring comes with the promise of new life.

Learn to lean on God and trust on His promises. Have hope in Him and know He is always with you.

The Shepherd and the Sheep

Bible Verse: {Jesus said} "My sheep listen to My voice; I know them, and they follow Me. I give them eternal life and they shall never perish; no one can snatch them out of my Father's hand. I and the Father are one." John 10:27-30

Something to Think About: Giving your heart to Jesus makes you his sheep. Sound kind of like a fairy tale or kid's story doesn't it? People becoming sheep, how silly. But that is not what this is about. Consider this story.

Bart was a shepherd many years ago. His job required him to watch a flock of two hundred sheep and keep them safe. He had to led them through their pasture and make sure none were lost.

On a bright sunny day, his cousin, Ramon, decided to walk with him as he drove the sheep to a different part of the pasture a good distance off. The task was going to take from sunrise to sunset and Ramon didn't want Bart to be lonely. Besides, they hadn't seen one another in three years and it was a great time to catch up.

When they were about an hour from their destination, Bart did another hourly count of the sheep. All were accounted for so they continued on. Once they arrived in the new part of the pasture, the sheep scattered throughout, enjoying their new territory. As Bart and Ramon sat under a tree watching the happy sheep, Bart noticed a small, scraggly sheep was missing.

"Ramon, the little one is gone!" He screamed.

"Oh, come on Bart. It's not a big deal. You know as well as I do the little one is a hindrance. She is slower than the rest, she is ugly and her wool is thin and can't even be used for clothing. Something's been wrong with her and she doesn't even produce milk. She is useless so why worry about her. You are better off without her," Ramon insisted.

"You're right about a lot of that, but she is one of my sheep and you may not understand this but I love her. She is useful to me. She is the one who usually walks besides me, the one who lies by my feet at lunch time. She is my friend. I have to go find her," Bart insisted.

The first five hours after dark, Bart searched for the little sheep but she was no where to be found. The sky was turning overcast and threatening bad weather. Bart knew he couldn't just go home and get some rest, although he wanted to. He had to be back at the pasture by sunrise to care for the rest of the sheep, but instead of going home, he went looking for the little one. No matter how worthless others may have thought she was, Bart cared for her.

As the rain began pouring down in sheets and lightening lit up the sky, Bart continued searching. At last he found her. She was hidden amongst the thickest brush. She had gotten so far into the thicket she couldn't find her way out. Bart cut away branch after branch as the storm blew harder. Instead of giving up when he hit a rough patch, he looked around until he found another place he could cut. At last, he was able to get the little sheep out.

Once back at the pasture, the sun rose above the tall green trees. Dew shined like diamonds on the green grass. Bart prayed and thanked God for finding his little one.

"Hey Bart," Ramon interrupted. "One of your sheep gave birth last night and is doing well and at least three fourths of them look like they are going to give you a big harvest of wool this year. This is something to celebrate!" Ramon said with excitement.

"That is good news, but my little one coming home is the real reason for celebration!" Bart exclaimed with joy and happiness. His face beamed with radiance knowing his lost sheep was found.

Jesus is our Shepherd and we are His sheep. It doesn't matter how worthless we feel, we are still special to God, just as the little one was for Bart. We are loved and cared for and Jesus wants us to be found and come home. If you are lost wondering in the wilderness known as earthly life, come home to Jesus. He is waiting on you!

Prayer: Dear Heavenly Father, Thank You for being my Shepherd and caring for a little lost sheep like me. I may not be worthy in many ways, but you love me anyway. Watch over me and protect me and lead me home to be with You.
    ~Amen

Whom Shall I Fear?

Bible Verse: The Lord is my light and my salvation – whom shall I fear? The Lord is the stronghold of my life – of whom shall I be afraid? Psalm 27:1

Something to Think About: When I was a sophomore in High School, I had a health class taught by Mr. Brady*. He was a coach of the football team and obviously a partier in his personal time. I had no problem with that; what he did in his personal time was none of my business.

One topic in our discussions was alcohol and its effects on the body and mind. It was interesting to learn the facts and figures and how little it took for some to be considered legally drunk while for larger people, it took a lot more. I always thought that seemed unfair, but also understood how body weight affected the alcohol absorption just as it did with medicines.

The coach knew most of the kids in class from extra curricular activities and also knew they were partiers and no stranger to alcohol. I just sat and listened in disgust as much of the classroom talk was about parties and getting drunk and the antics that went along with it.

Mr. Brady asked my friend Jenn*, "How much does it take to get you drunk?" just as he had asked several others, who responded with laughter and an exact amount it took them.

"Um, I don't know. I don't drink!" She bravely replied. His reaction was not one of pride or encouragement, but one of laughter.

He asked a few others who also had the experience to answer with "oh three or four" or even "it takes me 8 beers", although I was sure that was an exaggeration.

The then came to my best friend, Sally*. "Sally, what's your answer?"

"I don't drink," was her firm reply. Once again the answer was met with laughter.

I sat behind Sally so my turn was next. I could feel my face getting red as I awaited the dreaded question. I was really wishing the fire alarm would go off or something would happen to get me out of the hot seat.

"Tina, what about you? Are you a drinker? How much does it take for you?" he asked, almost as if teasing. He knew Sally, Jenn and I were best friends so he wasn't surprised when I answered.

"I have never drank," I answered shyly but with pride deep inside myself.

Once again, laughter, but this time, it was Mr. Brady's solitary laugh, but the whole class joined in. I felt embarrassed and degraded. Instead of feeling like I was living right, I felt as if I were a social outcast, bound to be taunted and tortured the rest of my life.

Looking at the three of us, he teased, "Oh, the three goody two shoes of Oak Hill High School!" I felt my face turning even redder and noticed Sally and Jenn were turning red as well. I am not sure if we were more humiliated or more astounded and angry.

After consideration and talking to my youth director about how degraded I felt and what outcasts we had quickly became, I realized it just didn't matter. I had God on my side and was doing the right thing. If I was a Christian and leading my life the best I could, then that was what mattered. I understood if God is for me and He is my strength, who could be against me? What harm could Mr. Brady in my life if God was the One in control? It was a liberating and awesome feeling that I still carry with me twenty six years later.

If you are caught between doing what is right and what others want you to do, always follow God. He will not lead you astray. Remember, no one can truly hurt you if you have God and if you allow God to be your strength.

Prayer: Dear Heavenly Father, help me find Your path and do what You want me to do. Help me not care what others think and help me remember You are my strength and that is all I need.
~Amen

~This is a true story that happened to me. Names with * have been changed.~

Joy through Trials

Bible Verse: Consider it pure joy, my brothers, whenever you face trials of many kinds, because you know that the testing of your faith develops perseverance. Perseverance must finish its work so that you may be mature and complete, not lacking anything. James 1:2-4

Something to Think About: At sixteen, Ollie was excited to finally have his driver's license and even more excited when his dad bought him a car for his birthday. His biggest concerns were who to take to Homecoming Dance, where to go to dinner on Friday night after the big game and which jeans looked best with his blue shirt he just bought. He was happy and carefree until the day he went to the doctor. He had been loosing some weight and was tired a lot lately, but he thought it was due to staying up late studying for exams, and if he told the truth, texting the girl he had a crush on, but his mother insisted he go.

The doctor told them the devastating news.

"Ollie, your test results are in and I am so sorry, but you have cancer," Dr. Morgan said sympathetically.

"Cancer? I can't have cancer. That's for old people who have smoked too much all their lives. Teens don't get cancer." Ollie laughed as he said it, but inside, his fear was taking over.

"This is a curable cancer, Ollie. You can beat this, but it's going to be very hard on you. First you will have to have surgery, and then we will start treatment. The chemotherapy and the radiation are really rough, but we caught the cancer early enough and I have no doubt you will beat it," Dr. Morgan told him confidently.

The surgery wasn't too bad. Ollie felt a little sore and was very tired, but nothing he couldn't handle. Then the chemotherapy and radiation began.

Ollie had always been a strong Christian and believed deeply in the Lord. When the chemo and radiation began, he trusted God to pull him through. He knew God would not let him down. Others may struggle through it and feel horrible, but they didn't have faith in God. He would be different.

The first three days of treatment, Ollie felt incredibly tired. He could barely get out of bed, but he was expecting that. He prayed, "Dear Lord, this isn't too bad. Thank You for helping me and thank you for keeping me from getting so sick and losing my hair like the doctor said I would. I have faith in You and know You will cure me and I will be fine. Amen".

After the fourth day, Ollie was brushing his wavy, thick hair when he noticed a large clump in his hands. It was just the beginning. Every day more hair was falling out and soon he had large bald spots in his head and the shiny, thick waves were now thin and dull.

After the fifth day of chemo, he came home and went to bed. After lying there an hour, he started feeling sick at this stomach. He barely made it to the restroom. "God, I know You will keep this sickness from me" he said over and over. Suddenly, the room began spinning and for the next six hours Ollie alternated between violently throwing up and lying on the cold tile bathroom floor. He never imagined being this sick. Throughout the next three months of treatment, Ollie felt like this.

"God, why are You doing this to me? Why? Have I not listened to You? What have I done that is so wrong? Are you even listening to me?" he asked God.

His faith was being tested every day. Some days he stayed strong and knew God would bring him through, but some days, when the sickness overtook him and he couldn't lift his head up off the toilet seat, he questioned if God even existed. Throughout his continuous prayer and devotions, reading whenever he felt well enough, his faith was once again found and he was stronger in the Lord.

Many times we believe we have strong faith, but then something happens and we question God. We question if He really loves us or even if He is really there. How could a God who claims to love us let us struggle and hurt as we often do? But through prayer, we can find our faith once again and learn to become even stronger in Christ.

When you are tempted to let go of your faith, hang in there and remember, fighting temptation and questioning your faith can lead to a more mature, close relationship with God, if you let it.

Prayer: Dear Heavenly Father, when I feel my faith slipping and I question You, please remain close to me. Help my trials lead me to a closer relationship with You and allow me to use my struggles and heartaches to develop a more mature relationship with You.
    ~Amen

Peace with God

Bible Verse: Therefore, since we have been justified through faith, we have peace with God through our Lord Jesus Christ, through whom we have gained access by faith into this grace in which we now stand. And we rejoice in the hope of the glory of God. Romans 5:1-2

Something to Think About: A terrible storm blew through the small town. Winds were strong, blowing over trees and knocking out the power. Thunder boomed loud enough to shake the house. The lightening strikes looked as if they could bolt right through the front window. David's parents and his little sister, Sara, were terrified, but David sat quietly reading by candlelight.

"David, what's wrong with you? Aren't you afraid?" Sara asked him.

"Honey, it's ok. This will be over soon," Mom stated nervously. Although she tried to appear calm, it was clear she was scared as well.

"Guys, it's just a storm!" David exclaimed.

"Yeah, a storm that could rip our house apart!" Sara cried.

"Do you remember at church when Pastor Rob spoke about the disciples being terrified out on the raging oceans and Jesus asking them where their faith was?" David asked.

"Yeah, I remember, but that was a long time ago. It doesn't help us now!" Sara stated and Mom and Dad silently agreed.

"Do you believe Jesus is still with us and still the same as He always was? Doesn't the Bible say 'Jesus is the same yesterday, today and tomorrow'? He asked them.

"Yes but…" Dad said. He was cut off by David's interruption.

"Then why are you so worried? God will protect us. He is with us right now. Trust in Him," David said.

Although Sara, Mom and Dad were still nervous, they knew David was right. They had to trust in Jesus and knew He was with them.

Many times in life we get scared. It is hard not to. Winds blow. Thunder booms. Rain causes floods. Bad people exist. People die. It is hard not to worry about those things and hard not to be afraid; however, in the middle of the fear, you must find strength and find your hope in Jesus Christ. Trust in Him and don't be afraid!

Prayer: Dear Heavenly Father, please help me when I am afraid. Help me remember You are with me and You will never leave me. Help me keep my peace I have in You, even in the toughest, scariest times.
    ~Amen

"Pray Also for Me"

Bible Verse: Pray also for me, that whenever I open my mouth, words may be given so that I will fearlessly make known the mystery of the gospel, for which I am an ambassador in chains. Pray that I may declare it fearlessly, as I should. Ephesians 6;19-20

Something to Think About: Roberto had never heard of Jesus or His love. His friend, Alejandra, was raised in church and lived a Christian life. She wanted nothing more than to share the good news with Roberto, but she didn't know how.

As she talked, the words sounded all wrong and Roberto was more confused than before. He just couldn't understand who Jesus was or why someone who lived so many years ago was important to him and Alejandra just couldn't explain.

That night, Alejandra prayed, "Dear Lord, please give me the words so I can explain You to Roberto and teach him about Your love. He doesn't know You and I want to introduce him to You. Please help me Lord. Amen."

The next day, Roberto began asking a few questions he asked the day before. Today, however, Alejandra answered every question with knowledge and confidence. Roberto began to understand. He didn't learn everything overnight, but after some time passed, he began going to church with Alejandra. Within six months, Roberto gave his life to Jesus and found the peace he had been looking for.

We are called to be witnesses for the Lord. Sometimes it is hard to know what to say or where to begin. Ask Jesus to guide you and give you the words to say that you may witness to others and help them find their way to the Lord.

Prayer: Dear Heavenly Father, Thank You for the opportunity to share Your word with others. I pray You give me the right words to speak and let only positive words come from my mouth. Teach me to be a disciple for You. Let my words come from You.
    ~Amen

Forgiveness

Forgiveness

Everyone sins. It is a fact of life. But what do you do after you have done something terrible, something you are sure God will never forgive you for? How do you let go of the guild you feel? How do you find your freedom in God?

This chapter will help you accept Christ's forgiveness. He died on a cross at Calvary to save us all from our sins, even you and me. As you read through this chapter, try to focus. Think of things you have done that you still blame yourself for, and then give them to God. Ask Him to forgive you. He will cleanse you and you will be able to look to the future instead of reliving and regretting yesterday.

Asking God's Forgiveness

Bible Verse: How much more then, will the blood of Christ, who through the eternal Spirit offered himself unblemished to God, cleanse our consciences from acts that lead to death, so that we may serve the living God? Hebrews 9:14

Something to Think About: At a party he had not planned on attending, George drank too much. He never intended to drink, but his friends kept bugging him until he finally gave in. One beer led to another, then another and before he knew it, he was drunk. In his intoxicated state, George could not think clearly and told himself, "I am fine to drive."

As he backed out of the parking space, he didn't take time to look behind him. His best friend, Harry, was standing in the driveway talking to Amy. George's car came to a sudden stop. As he got out of the car, he was cursing, something else he didn't usually do. He thought his car was messing up again. Walking to the back of the car, he began screaming when he realized he had backed over Amy and Harry. Their mangled bodies were lying on the street, rain falling on their bloody, terrified faces. George immediately felt regret, sorrow and guilt for what he had done. The reality of the consequences of his drinking was far too real.

Amy is now paralyzed from her chest down and Harry's funeral was held three days after the accident. George feels more guilt and pain than he can express. He has become more solemn and withdrawn, doesn't talk to his friends and is failing his classes. He believes he did something so terrible, so unforgivable, even God will never be able to forgive him. That is not the case.

The blood of Jesus Christ, our Savior, is way bigger than anything you could ever do. His blood was shed to cleanse all your sins, no matter how small or how large. It doesn't matter if you sin is lying to Mom about finishing your homework or drinking alcohol and killing someone. He will forgive you. When He was on the cross, dying for our freedom from sin, He didn't say, "Well, I will die for your little, harmless sins, but if you do something really stupid or bad, then all bets are off. You're on your own." No, He said, "I will forgive **all** your sins.

If you do something terrible, you will still have to deal with the consequences because of your actions, but Jesus Christ will forgive you and erase the sins from your life if you ask Him, believe in Him and truly try to change. Before you read the prayer, think about all your sins, big ones and small ones. They are all the same to Jesus. Ask Him with all your heart for forgiveness. As long as you truly mean it, Jesus will forgive you.

Prayer: Dear Heavenly Father, Thank You for loving me. I have done a lot wrong and I feel terrible about it. I realize I am not perfect and I do make mistakes, but I know your love will set me free. Thank You for the blood You shed on Calvary so that my sins may be forgiven. I ask that you please forgive all my sins and set me free from the guilt I carry within myself. Help me learn from my mistakes and help me grow closer to you. Thank You for Your forgiveness.
~Amen

Forgiving and Letting Go of Bitterness and Anger

Bible Verse: Get rid of all bitterness, rage and anger, brawling and slander, along with every form of malice. Ephesians 4:31

Something to Think About: Three years ago when Maria was a Sophomore, Jordan came to her house a lot to visit. He always said the sweetest things and led her to believe he truly cared about her. He was always polite to her parents and even her little brother and often brought her beef jerky, her favorite treat. He also called or texted several times a day.

He had visited most of the day Good Friday and even spent the night on the cough because he had worked hard all week and was too exhausted to drive home. Maria was ecstatic and was falling in love with the handsome young boy.

Easter Sunday, Maria texted him good morning, but he never replied. That evening she asked how his day had been, but once again, he didn't respond. Two days went by and she heard nothing. Another week and he still hadn't contacted her. After a month's time she had to admit to herself he wasn't just busy, he had left her and wasn't going to call again. She was hurt very deeply.

A few months later, Maria found out from a friend that Jordan was getting married. Her heart shattered as if it were glass hit by a boulder; however, Maria did not attack back, hold on to resentment or anger, nor did she say negative things. Maria simply said, "I wish him the best and hope he is happy." They weren't just words, it was how she truly felt. When she prayed, she didn't pray Jordan would be miserable or that his fiancé would break his heart, but prayed for his safety while he was in the military and prayed they would have a long and happy marriage.

It's been three years since Maria suffered the heart break from Jordan. When she sees him or hears about him, the pain is as fresh as if it just happened. She has accepted she will never stop loving him and there will always be a small tear in her heart, left by him.

Although Maria has been deeply hurt, she still wishes the best for Jordan. It would be so easy for her to hate him and wish him ill, but that's not who she is. This is exactly what the Lord wants us to do. Life is hard. People hurt us. They do bad things. It's so much easier to hold on to the bitterness and anger toward those who have hurt us, but that isn't what God wants. He wants us to give it to Him and for us to forgive. He knows how hard it is and how much we hurt. He isn't asking us to take the person back into our lives like nothing happened. He is telling us to let go of the anger and not strike back. We are to love the other person, but dislike their actions. It can be done, as Maria showed.

Prayer: Dear Heavenly Father, please help me get rid of anger, bitterness and malice in my heart. Please teach me to replace those feelings with love and kindness. Help me learn to let go of my pain and show kindness to those who have hurt me.
    ~Amen

*This is a true story. The girl, Maria, is my daughter, Emily, who I am extremely proud of for the way she has handled the heartache!

Forgiving Others

Bible Verse: For if you forgive men when they sin against you, your heavenly Father will also forgive you. But if you do not forgive men their sins, your Father will not forgive you your sins. Matthew 6:13-15

Something to Think About: Brandi had a huge crush on Michael. He was tall, really cute and had shaggy dark hair. When he looked at her, his eyes reminded her of a sad puppy dog. At lunch, Michael always sat with her and they flirted back and forth. He had even hinted he was going to ask her to the Prom.

Her best friend, Melanie, knew Brandi was crazy about Michael, but she still flirted with him. It hurt Brandi's feelings, but she didn't let it come between them.

A few weeks before Prom, Brandi was crushed when Melanie came running up to her locker exclaiming, "I asked Michael to go to the Prom and he said yes!"

Brandi was understandably hurt. Melanie apologized over and over, but Brandi refused to forgive her. Melanie even said she would break off the date and the two of them could spend the evening together. Brandi wanted nothing to with her. Over the summer, Brandi ignored all Melanie's phone calls and Melanie eventually gave up. A great friendship was lost over one mistake.

A week before school started, Brandi attended church. During the service, her preacher talked about forgiveness. The ride home was long and quiet and Brandi used the time to think and pray. God spoke to her and she realized she wasn't perfect and neither was Melanie. She also realized that if God could forgive all the mean things she had said recently to her mother then she should forgive Melanie as well.

After Brandi talked to Melanie, they each forgave one another and their friendship grew even stronger. The girls remained best friends through high school and are now attending the same college.

God grants us forgiveness through His mercy and love, not our actions. We can not "buy" His forgiveness. He expects us to the same when others fail us. It isn't always easy, but through prayer and God's help, you can forgive. You may always remember the event, but you can let go and give forgiveness. Let God help you.

Prayer: Dear Heavenly Father, Please help me when others have hurt me. Live through me and let your light shine that I may not hold resentment toward anyone. Teach me to forgive others just as you have forgiven me, no matter what they have done. I know it doesn't mean I have to forget or even be their friend anymore, but I can let go of the resentment. I can't do this alone, God. I need Your help. Guide me and help me grow.
~Amen

Forgiving Yourself

Bible Verse: "Their sins and lawless acts I will remember no more." Hebrew 8:12

Something to Think About: Lisa was only fifteen years old when she became serious with a guy named James, who was four years older than her. They dated for nine months and often went out alone on dates. James was patient and never pushed Lisa to have sex before she was ready, but he also encouraged her to do it. On a cool autumn day, Lisa gave in. Once they began a sexual relationship, it continued for another six months. At the time, Lisa was involved with her church youth group. Although she knew premarital sex was a sin, she avoided thinking about it in those terms.

After Lisa and James broke up, she spent a lot of time alone in her room. Her heart was broken and she needed time to heal. As she sat alone, she read her Bible, learning more about God's Word. A rush of emotion flowed through her as she realized her sexual activity had been a sinful act. She prayed for God's forgiveness and promised not to do it again.

A year later, Lisa started dating Danny. Their relationship quickly became sexual. Saturday nights they went out on a date to dinner or the movies and typically had sex before he brought her home. Most of the time, Lisa didn't really want to, but felt she owed it to Danny. Although she really liked him, she knew she wasn't really in love with him and there was no future, which fueled her guilt even further. On Sunday mornings, she would pray for forgiveness.

This cycle lasted for four years. She was promiscuous and seldom said no, even when she wanted to. Then, she felt the guilt weigh her down once again and asked God for forgiveness.

Several years later Lisa was married and had a beautiful baby girl. She was happier than she ever dreamed. Her happily ever after with her prince charming and her little princess were no longer only a dream, but a reality. Lisa often found herself in tears of joy thinking of her wonderful life. But some nights, she remembered her tainted past and the guilt came flooding back, just as if she were still sixteen years old. Although she knew God had forgiven her, she still hadn't forgiven herself. The guilt ate away at her, keeping her from truly feeling God's love and from completely enjoying her family.

The Bible tells us Jesus will not remember our sins, but it is often hard for us to forget. We tend to believe, "if I haven't forgiven myself, how can Jesus forgive me?" The answer is really simple. He is perfect, we aren't. If you are holding onto the constant memory of something you have done wrong, please take a moment to think about Jesus. Let His healing power heal you. Give it to Him and trust in His Word. Trust that your sin is forgiven and forgotten, just as if it never even happened. Sure, you may have to live with the consequences and you may have to work hard to overcome obstacles, but with Christ's help, you do that. He no longer remembers your sin, so why should you? Use your mistakes to learn by.

Prayer: Dear Heavenly Father, I am holding onto my own sins. I know you have forgiven me, but I haven't forgiven myself. Please teach me to let go of my past, to learn from it and to use it to grow closer to you.
~Amen

Saved By Grace

For God so Loved the World

Bible Verse: {Jesus said} "For God so loved the world that he gave his one and only Son, so that whoever believes in Him shall not perish but have eternal life." John 3:16

Something to Think About: We learn from this verse how much God loves us. He loves us enough that He allowed His **only** Son to die a brutal, tortuous death on a cross, just so that we may have our sins forgiveness.

God does not say, "I love some of you in the world enough, but some of you aren't worth it." He says He loves the world. That means every single one of us, no matter how insignificant we may think we are or how much we have sinned. God loves everyone. No one is left out.

The last part of the verse says whoever believes in Him shall not perish but have eternal life. Does that mean if you believe in Jesus you will never die and you will live forever? The answer is no…and yes. You will not live your earthly life forever. As long as our bodies are on this earth we will have pain and illness accidents and murders, etc. You may live to be fifteen or one hundred and one, but the fact is one day your body will die. The good news is if you believe in Jesus Christ and are a Christian, your soul will never die. You will spend eternity, not just a few hours, days or even years, but eternity, with Jesus Christ. Now that is good news!

Prayer: Dear Heavenly Father, Thank You for loving the world enough to give us Your only Son. That is a gift I will never be able to repay, but I know all you ask in return is for me to love You and to live for You. When I am feeling down and lonely, please help me remember how much You love me. Help me as I move along my Christian journey and lead and guide me so I am closer to You.
    ~Amen

The Way, the Truth and the Life

Bible Verse: Jesus answered, "I am the way and the truth and the life. No one comes to the Father except through Me. If you really knew Me, you would know My Father as well. From now on, you do know Him and have seen Him." John 14:6

Something to Think About: There are choices everywhere. Should I choose Coke or Pepsi or maybe Dr. Pepper? Should I go to the movies or out to dinner? Should I go to the beach or stay home and read? Should I wear the blue shoes or the red ones? Today more than anytime in the past we are overwhelmed with choices.

One thing we do not have a choice about is how to be forgiven by God. We don't have to sit and wonder which is the best way or if we made the right decision, because there is only **one** way.

Jesus tells us He is the way. He doesn't say, "Hey I am the best way, but there are other ways you could try if ya want." He says, "I am **THE** way!" If you know Jesus, then You know God, because Jesus is the way to God.

Prayer: Dear Heavenly Father, Thank You for Jesus and for Him being the way to You. Thank You that through Him my sins are forgiven. Thank You for sending Jesus as my way, my truth and my life.
    ~Amen

Saved by Grace

Bible Verse: For it is by grace you have been saved, through faith—and this not from yourselves, it is the gift of God—not by works, so that no one can boast. Ephesians 2:8-9

Something to Think About: At lunch, Mary Alice and Dre got into an argument about being saved and God's forgiveness.

"No Mary Alice, you are wrong. You can not be saved unless you do good things," Dre demanded.

"Yes you can. All it takes to be forgiven is for you to ask and to love God. You can't buy forgiveness!" Mary Alice told him.

"Look at Mother Theresa. She did good things all the time so she was forgiven and went to heaven. That's how it's done. You do good things for others and bam, you are saved and go to heaven when you die," Dre told her.

"Dre, you really need to read your Bible better. We aren't saved by what we do. We are saved by God's grace. He loves us no matter what and if we love Him and ask for forgiveness He gives it to us. We are all sinners and no matter what good things we do, they won't erase our sins. Only His grace does that," she replied.

Dre thought for a moment, then asked, "Are you saying no matter what I do or who I am or who I help, I am still going to sin?"

"Yes. Everyone does. It's part of being human."

"Then what's the point in even trying?" he asked sadly.

"The point is we try to do our best because we want to honor God. We want to help others because we love Him and we love others, not to gain forgiveness. His grace flows to us because of the blood Jesus shed for us. That's what God is all about!" she told him.

"Wow, you are really giving me hope I never had before. I always thought before when I did something wrong I was going straight to hell. I didn't know His love was always there. Will you teach me more and help me find where to read?" he asked.

"I would love to. Come over tonight after school and we will get started. Bring a friend if ya want!" Mary Alice replied with excitement.

Sometimes it feels we do so much wrong God can't love us. But that isn't the case. He loves us no matter what we do. If we do good things like feeding the hungry or leading others to God, that doesn't mean we are forgiven. It takes God's mercy and our asking Him for forgiveness. Still do good things to please God, but remember to ask his forgiveness and let His grace free you from your sins.

Prayer: Dear Heavenly Father, Thank You for Your grace and Your forgiveness. Thank You for loving me even when I do wrong things. I know that it is Your grace and the blood of Jesus that saves me, not Your work. Help me do good things to honor You, and help me remember to ask forgiveness for my sins. You are amazing, Dear Lord and I love You.
~Amen

Salvation in Jesus Christ

You hear about it in church and hear friends talking about "Salvation". But what exactly does that mean?

Salvation means being saved. As you have learned through the study of this devotional book, there is only one way to be saved, and that is through the blood of Jesus Christ.

"Through the blood of Jesus? Does that mean I have to drink His blood or bath in it?" you may ask after hearing about it during Communion at church. You drink the blood Jesus, "eat this (cracker) in remembrance of me" and sing "washed in the blood of the Lamb." The answer is yes, and no. Figuratively, yes you do. His blood washes away our sins, so as we drink the wine, we picture his blood washing away our sins and cleansing us. When you do communion, you drink either grape juice or wine, depending on your church's beliefs and practices. You eat crackers or bread to symbolize the body of Christ, so He is always a part of you. Literally, no you don't have to do it. It would be gross literally drinking someone's blood, even Jesus'. Only in demented horror movies do we see anyone actually eating someone's flesh. And taking a literal bath in blood would be very cleansing would it? God knows this. He doesn't want you do to it literally, but wants you to realize His blood is what freed you from your sins.

Jesus died on the cross at Calvary to set you free. The blood He shed grants us God's mercy and forgiveness. Before Christ's death, sacrifices such as lambs, were offered to God to gain forgiveness and for requests. One could not possibly have a conversation with God without a sacrifice and going through a priest. Jesus stopped that. He is the Lamb of God, meaning He was the ultimate and final sacrifice. He died so that you may be forgiven, just by asking. Pretty awesome isn't it?

Since Jesus made the sacrifice, you are now free to go to God for anything without going through a higher priest of offering sacrifices Jesus is the High Priest and He made the final sacrifice. You can talk to God without being afraid, without feeling like a nobody or feeling like a failure. It doesn't matter how you pray. Perhaps having an informal conversation with him while you shower in the mornings is your best way to communicate. Maybe you prefer the more formal prayers. It doesn't matter. Just talk. He wants to be your Father and your best friend. He is there and loves you. He wants you to tell Him what's buggin' you and what you need help with. He wants you to talk to him everyday. He is the extreme BFF.

Now that you know you can go to Him anytime because of Jesus' sacrifice, you may still be asking what it means to be saved and how you go about doing it. It's really quite easy, although adults sometimes seem to make it more difficult and confusing. All you have to do ask for God's forgiveness and it's yours. Of course, He wants you to change and wants you to do better, but He doesn't walk away when you slip up and do something wrong. If He did, there would be no Christians, because everyone slips up. You also have to believe in Jesus Christ and love Him with all your heart.

So that's it. Love Him and ask for forgiveness!

If you are not a Chrsitian, what is holding you back? Are you afraid of God? Are you afraid you can't be all He wants you to be? No one is all God wants them to be. Remember, Christianity is a journey and well fall short of His desires for us, but He will never turn away from you. He loves you!

What else is keeping you from it? Are you afraid of what your friends or classmates will say? Don't worry about them; this is your life not theirs. Be an example to them, not a follower. Follow Jesus, not your classmates.

Are you afraid God will ask too much of you? He won't. He may ask a lot of you, but what He asks are all things He knows you can do. He knows you better than anyone else does, even better than you know yourself.

This is a big step in your life. When you are ready, ask God to forgive you. He's waiting on you to come to Him. He won't push you or beg you. He will just wait patiently until you call upon Him.

About the Author

Tina Toler is a mother of four children and is recently married to Larry Keel. She was born and raised in West Virginia. She moved to Southern North Carolina summer of 2006. She has a degree in Business Management, but decided on a career in writing.

She is working for a non-profit magazine, "Divinity Girlz" and is looking forward to helping lead others to God. She is currently revising her first fictional novel and has begun her second.

To contact Ms. Toler, you may follow her on Twitter at http://www.twitter.com/tinatoler , or email her at tinatoler@yahoo.com. Her website is www.tinatolerkeel.com. She is also author and founder of a LGBT site, www.itswhoiam.org that provides help and support to teens and their families.

Made in the USA
Columbia, SC
14 January 2022